CHRISTINA BAGLIVI

NORTHERN ITALY

A TASTE OF TRATTORIA

Maps by Kevin Tinglof

Mustang Publishing Co.
Memphis, TN

Distributed to the trade in the U.S.A. by National Book
Network, Lanham, MD. Distributed in England and Europe by Gazelle Book Services, Lancaster, England. For
information on distribution elsewhere, please contact
Mustang Publishing.

Library of Congress Cataloging-in-Publication Data

Baglivi, Christina.
    Northern Italy : a taste of trattoria / Christina
  Baglivi ; maps by Kevin Tinglof.
        p.   cm.
    Includes index.
    ISBN 0-914457-43-8 (alk. paper : pbk.) : $9.95
    1. Restaurants, lunch rooms, etc.--Italy,
  Northern--Guide-books. 2. Italy, Northern--
  Description and travel--1975-   --Guide-books.
  I. Title.
    TX907.5.I82N63   1991
    647.9545--dc20   90-50864
                                                  CIP

Printed on acid-free paper.

10 9 8 7 6 5 4 3 2 1

For Kevin,
my favorite dinner companion

Contents

Introduction

Before my husband Kevin and I boarded the plane to Italy, my Uncle Giorgio took me aside. In his eternal Italian accent he said, "Forget eating in *ristoranti*—they're too expensive for your budget. Instead, see the real Italy, and eat where Italians eat: *trattorie*."

We took my uncle's advice; so should you. This book is filled with those honest eateries and the specialty dishes they're renowned for. Look past the mismatched silverware and chipped plates to discover what Italians have known for years—family-run *trattorie* offer simple, delicious, regional dishes at inexpensive prices. In these little dining spots, two can feast on many courses, with plenty of wine, for **half** the cost of a typical *ristorante*.

The problem with *trattorie* is that finding them is like playing "Hide and Seek." The finest ones, frequented by locals, are hidden in residential neighborhoods, off the tourist track. We followed the aroma of garlic down side streets, under laundry lines strung across alleyways, and past TVs blaring soccer games. Often, sandwiched between a meat market and fruit stand, in a small *piazza*, we'd find a bright awning with our favorite new word—*Trattoria!* Prices on the menu posted outside told us if the establishment was economically suitable for us.

The majority of patrons are casually dressed families, often with infants and grandparents in tow. Young children inevitably fall asleep in their chairs, while the adults continue to talk, laugh, and sing till closing time. It's not unusual for the owner, who is probably the chef, to bring out *Sambuca* and share a late sip of the strong, licorice-tasting liquor.

Money Matters

In each *trattoria* review we list two charges that may be added to your bill, regardless of what you order. However, these charges vary from place to place. **Pane e coperto** (cover charge) means: "If you sit down and we bring bread to your table, we'll charge you." The cost is about 2,000 lire per person. The second charge, **servizio** (service charge or tip), runs 10%-15%, but many *trattorie* omit it. An Italian friend explained *servizio* by saying: "Italians are not big tippers. So, restaurant owners in tourist cities add the service charge because they know Americans will pay it."

So how does a traveler know what's proper? If the cover charge is big—2,000 lire or more—the restaurant owner is estimating the tip and getting it up front. If it's less, and if the service is good, feel free to leave extra lire. When in doubt, watch the Italian diners and follow their lead.

Follow the Crowd—With the Maps

After a *trattoria* passed our price test, we analyzed the clientele inside. A large crowd, shouting and gesturing, is always a good sign. I'm convinced that for a *trattoria* to have exceptional food, the customers must be Italian—they know their restaurants. So, don't be shy about asking a native for his favorite *trattoria*. The owner of our *pensione* in Rome confided, "Try Pasqualino's across the street. It's very good and not much money." The food, service, and atmosphere were so wonderful, we ate there three nights in a row.

Our investigative work had its flaws, though. During a visit to Venice, we sampled a dozen *trattorie* and foolishly relied on our sense of direction to lead us back for a follow-up meal. When we tried to return, we ended up lost in the city's web of canals. Instead of a bowl of steaming *minestrone*, we ate in silence at Wendy's. We learned our lesson, and that's why a map accompanies each review.

Hours and Accessibility

Every establishment closes one day a week and one month a year, but each *trattoria* is different. Since there's nothing more frustrating than searching for one and finding it closed, note the days and hours of operation in every review.

Most *trattorie* are housed in old buildings with long, narrow staircases. Unfortunately, none in this book is equipped with ramps, rails, or elevators for the disabled. However, some *trattorie* are located on the ground floor with no large steps to cross, and, with a little help, you could easily navigate a wheel chair into the dining area. I've labeled such eateries as "Wheel chair negotiable" and added the symbol ♿.

Regional Differences

While Italy's *ristoranti* have homogenized their menus to incorporate dishes from every part of the country, *trattorie* cook specialties only from their region. That's why you'll find wonderful *pesto* served in *trattorie* in the northern, herb-growing area of Liguria, but you'll rarely find it in a Naples eatery.

The land and climate sets the North apart from the South (Rome is the dividing point). In the North, lush grasslands and cool temperatures provide an environment perfect for animal products used in their cooking: butter, lard, *prosciutto* (ham), and *pancetta* (bacon). Northerners also cook with a lot of rice, while pasta is the southern staple.

Eating Habits

Unlike Americans, Italians don't eat a big breakfast. A cup of *cappuccino* and a chunk of unbuttered bread—often left from dinner the night before—is standard morning fare, usually consumed standing at the counter of a local bar (which is as much an eating bar as a drinking bar).

For lunch, there's a saying: "Rush hour in Italy is noon, when workers speed home before their pasta gets cold!" A nap follows the midday meal, and businesses usually close in early afternoon.

The social highlight of the evening is dinner, and eating after 8:00pm is standard. Long after the sun sets, locals meander to their favorite *trattoria*, spending hours at the table, conversing with friends, savoring the food and wine. Portions in *trattoria* are smaller than in U.S. restaurants, but this lets you sample many courses rather than fill up on one large entrée.

I knew Europeans ate late, but I never realized how slowly Italians dine, carefully deciding after each course what they want next. In Rome, we found a *trattoria* near the Pantheon. Though there were many tables outside, not one was vacant. As we began to walk away, an elderly waiter in a long white apron (wrapped around a huge pot belly) grabbed my arm. He pulled me toward another waiter setting up a folding table in front of a door. Motioning for us to sit, he shoved menus in our hands and walked off. Moments later, he returned, took our order for *antipasto*, and walked away again, this time mumbling something.

Confused, I asked Kevin, "Why didn't he take the rest of our order?"

"I'm pretty sure his mumbling was, 'That's all for now'," Kevin said. "I guess he'll take our pasta order after he brings the appetizer."

And Kevin was right. After each course, Luigi offered suggestions for the next one. That night, eating became "dining." From then on, three-hour dinners were common for us. Feeling like true natives, we'd watch the people stroll by, inhale the intoxicating aromas from the food around us, and sip great Italian wine.

Wine

Few middle-class Italians drink bottled wine; it's too expensive. Instead, house wine (*vino della casa*—a term you'll commit to memory) is the popular beverage. Since "jug wine" is produced locally, it's an economical choice. Don't be afraid you're missing out by not ordering a familiar brand name. Italian house wine will please even the most discriminating palate.

Finally . . .
I sincerely hope you find *Northern Italy: A Taste of Trattoria* a useful, delicious, money-saving reference. Even more, though, I hope it will inspire you to follow your own nose and taste buds and discover *trattorie* for yourself. If they're wonderful, please let me know about them!

For now, let me show you the best way to experience Italy, her people, and her culinary feasts—for a price any traveler can afford.

Buon appetito!

Disclaimer

As you plan your trip with this guide, please remember that some things probably have changed. Though the book was as accurate as possible at publication, it's inevitable that some *trattorie* will close, hours will vary, and prices will rise. Always try to call ahead to confirm specific details. We accept no responsibility for any problems you encounter as a result of an inaccuracy in this book.

Of course, if you do find an error—or if you'd like to criticize or praise our effort—we'd love to hear from you. Write us in care of Mustang Publishing, P.O. Box 3004, Memphis, TN 38173, U.S.A.

The Region of Latium

Three-fifths of Latium's five million people live in the dominant capital city, Rome, where culinary trends are set and where eating habits seem to revolve around days or events of the week. If it's Thursday, *gnocchi di semolino*, tiny dumplings tossed in grated *parmigiano* cheese, are sure to be *il piatto del giorno* (the special of the day) at many *trattorie*. On Sunday, the aroma of *trippa alla romana* (tripe simmered in tomato sauce) catches everyone's attention. And if pancakes arrive at the breakfast table, it's undoubtedly St. Joseph's Day.

Latium prides itself on its vegetables. The countryside surrounding the Eternal City is mostly volcanic land, and the soil, rich in minerals and nutrients, enhances the appearance and taste of everything that grows. Though fields of peas, beans, celery, and lettuce blanket nearby Alban Hills, the artichoke (*carciofo*) is the highest-rated vegetable among Romans. Served grilled (*alla giudia*), deep fried (*al tegame*), or boiled with garlic (*alla romana*), they're always delicious and popular.

The Campo dei Fiori, Rome's largest outdoor market, is a cornucopia for chefs and housewives on the prowl for fresh produce, and it's a social center for locals anxious to exchange neighborhood gossip.

Romans take their time when they dine out—they're big on conversation and appetizers. They can sit for hours at a table without ordering their meal. Instead, they munch on *pinzimonio*, a platter of fresh, raw vegetables with a bowl of olive oil seasoned with salt and pepper for dipping, and *bruschetta* (garlic bread).

THE REGION OF

ATIUM

Romans also take their spaghetti seriously. Two specialties topping the list of favorites are *spaghetti all'amatriciana* (pasta tossed with onions, bacon, tomatoes and white wine) and *carbonara* (pasta with a rich, bacon/cream sauce).

Latium's vineyards benefit from the soil, too. The chief grape-growing area is around an extinct volcano, Lake Bolsena. Local table wines, from vineyards like *Frascati* and *Est! Est! Est!* are light, dry white wines—delicious and inexpensive complements to any feast.

Rome is the best city to start an Italian holiday. The friendly, casual nature of the locals makes dining and touring a delight. In summer, *trattoria* owners pull tables from hot, stuffy dining rooms out to the sidewalks. People parade by and seek out old friends. If none can be found, they'll make new ones from the diners enjoying the balmy evening and home-style meal.

THE REGION OF
LATIUM

N ↑

VIA DEL CINQUE

VIA DELLA PELLICCIA

■
DA CORRADO

VIA P. PAGLIA

PIAZZA SANTA MARIA
IN TRASTEVERE

CENTRO ↗

DA CORRADO

ROME

Da Corrado

Via della Pelliccia, 39
Rome
Phone: 580-6004
Hours: noon-3:00pm, 7:00pm-10:00pm. Closed
   Sunday.
Cover charge: 800 lire/person. No service charge.
Cost of our meal: 28,900 lire
Wheel chair negotiable. &

Hardly noticeable, hidden in a tiny storefront north of
the Piazza Santa Maria in Rome's Trastevere quarter,
Da Corrado is like an unmade bed—a little unattrac-
tive to look at, but warm and comfortable under the
covers.

As Kevin and I enter, the moist air—coming from the
kitchen concealed behind a steamed-up, glass
partition—gives way to inviting smells of garlic and
herbs. We take our seats and scrape one shoe against
the other, to remove the sawdust from the floor. Tubes
of fluorescent lights hang bare on the wall, highlighting a garage-sale display of posters, photos, and girlie
calendars.

With a cigarette in one hand, the owner tosses two
wine glasses and an ashtray on our weathered table.
Don't let his gruff exterior and deep voice fool you; he's
really a nice guy, willing to explain unfamiliar-sounding
words.

From his short, verbal listing, I choose my first
course: *bucatini all'amatriciana*, a Roman favorite—
long, hollow macaroni with tomato sauce, flavored with
pieces of bacon and white wine. Kevin orders *ravioli*
filled with fresh ricotta cheese and chopped spinach,
topped with tomato sauce.

All afternoon, locals come and go—businessmen, construction workers, students, and even four old ladies who consume two liters of house wine easily. We could, too—the white, dry *Frascati* is light on the palate, but we show control and order a half-carafe.

For seconds, we have *spezzatino bianco*—several sautéed chunks of veal in a white wine sauce, accompanied by lots of roasted potatoes—and *pizzaiola*—not a pizza, but it does require extra bread to sop up the excess, zesty tomato sauce covering thin slices of veal.

Da Corrado is the best deal we found in Rome. Though it lacks style, it's brimming with local color— no tourists here, just good Roman fare, dirt-cheap.

Trattoria Mezzaluna

Via Cardinale Marmaggi, 12
Rome
Phone: 582-612
Hours: 12:30pm-3:00pm, 7:30pm-11:00pm. Closed
   Monday.
Cover charge: 2,000 lire/person. No service charge.
Cost of our meal: 33,000 lire
Wheel chair negotiable. &

On Sunday mornings in Rome, vendors fill the banks
of the Tiber River, selling everything from badly imi-
tated American jeans to kitchen items and antiques.
Kevin and I stroll among the crowds for hours, listening
to sales-pitches: "All shirts only 2,000 lire!" they shout
from tabletops.

By noon, we're in the Trastevere, a neighborhood
southwest of the historic center. Directly off the busy,
main boulevard of Viale Trastevere is Trattoria Mezzaluna. Outside, anchored in a "No Parking Zone," four tables are surrounded by potted shrubs for an *al frésco*
feeling. We go inside to sit in the small dining room,
among tables and heavy, wood-backed benches.

Today's vegetables—a tureen filled with exotic salad
greens, string beans with lemon, sautéed cauliflower
and spinach, and grilled eggplant—are displayed on the
front counter, in full view of diners. With a half-carafe
of *Rosatello Ruffino*, one of Latium's favorite red wines,
comes a basket of thickly sliced, warm bread.

We start with a beloved Roman specialty—*spaghetti
carbonara*, pasta tossed with cream, eggs, and crum-
bled bacon. Trattoria Mezzaluna adds lots of freshly
ground pepper, and we add grated *parmigiano* cheese
because we can't get enough!

THE REGION OF
LATIUM

N ↑

CENTRO ↗

PIAZZA
S. SONNINO

VIA D. FRATTE DI TR.

VIALE TRASTEVERE

VIA C. MARMAGGI

MEZZALUNA ↰

PIAZZA
MASTAI

RATTORIA MEZZALUNA

ROME

For a second course, we order *vitello al forno*, slices of baked veal seasoned with rosemary and served in a sauce of light, balsamic vinegar and olive oil.

The vegetables on the front counter have been drawing my attention all afternoon, and I decide on *melanzane ai ferri*, thin slices of eggplant grilled in a touch of bacon fat for a slightly smoky flavor, then sprinkled with chopped parsley, olive oil, and balsamic vinegar—a perfect accompaniment to this feast.

It's standing room only as we leave the tiny eatery. I guess the Tiber-side vendors and their shoppers have taken a break from selling and buying to have some great Roman cuisine.

THE REGION OF
LATIUM

N

VIA LABICANA

PIAZZA
DEL COLOSSEO

COLOSSEUM

VIA CLAUDIA

PASQUALINO

VIA OSTILIA

VIA SS. QUATTRO

RATTORIA PASQUALINO

ROME

Trattoria Pasqualino

Via SS. Quattro, 66
Rome
Phone: 735-903
Hours: noon-2:30pm, 7:00pm-midnight. Closed
   Monday.
Cover charge: 2,000 lire/person. No service charge.
Cost of our meal: 37,500 lire
Wheel chair negotiable. &

As I turn the corner, I spy eight linen-covered tables
lining the sidewalk and waiters in black tie parading past
with long, white napkins folded over their forearms.
It's Trattoria Pasqualino, exactly as Kevin and I left it
four years earlier, when it was recommended by the
owner of Colosseum Residenza, a tiny *pensione* across
the street. The *pensione* is gone, but Pasqualino's and
the memory of long, romantic dinners remain.

   One block from the Colosseum in a quiet neighborhood, Pasqualino's is truly a local eatery. Everyone who
walks through the door, past the counter filled with
tempting pastries and a huge basket of *porcini*
mushrooms, is greeted like an old friend. They even
seem to remember us.

   I take a seat facing the ancient stadium, now silhou-
etted by a nearly full moon. Kevin orders our favorite
house wine—*Frascati*, a dry white from the nearby area
of Castelli.

   There are a few additions to the menu since our last
visit, and we curiously try two. Kevin approves of his
fettuccine pasqualino—a newly popular house specialty
of homemade noodles in a tomato, champagne, and
spiced ground meat sauce. My *fettuccine al salmone* has
those celebrated, long, flat noodles that Romans love

so much—tossed in a smoked salmon *rose* (tomatoes and cream sauce).

After all these years I recognize the short, gray-haired waiter who sings Italian folk songs while he sets tables. But not everything is the same. The eatery has expanded, adding an upstairs dining room to accommodate a growing, regular clientele. And there are new, large bathrooms.

For our second course, we repeat a dish we had during our first sojourn—*galletto alla diavola*, grilled water hen spiced "like the devil." Actually, it's mild, but just as delicious and juicy as I remembered. And we can't resist ordering *carciofo alla romana*—a Roman specialty of boiled artichokes with lots of garlic.

We marvel at the way Pasqualino's has managed to stay humble, well-priced, and palatable, despite its increased business. Kevin and I look forward to our next visit, when we can once again sit in the shadow of the Colosseum and dine on good Roman food.

Trattoria Agustarello

Via Giovanni Branca, 100
Rome
Phone: 576-6585
Hours: 12:30pm-3:00pm, 7:30pm-midnight. Closed
  Sunday.
Cover charge: 2,000 lire/person.
Service charge: 10%
Cost of our meal: 46,000 lire
Wheel chair negotiable. ♿

Rome still has traditional *trattorie* that offer good,
regional cuisine at fair prices. The trick is to leave the
city center and the historic district. After a morning exploring the Forum, Kevin and I walk south along the
Tiber until we hit Testaccio, a lively neighborhood near
the Aventino area.

At first, we don't notice Trattoria Agustarello. There's
no awning, no flashing neon sign, and no menu posted
outside. But the noise from the crowded dining room
and an aroma of tomato sauce lure us in for lunch. The
decor is simple and uncomplicated—one large room
with crown molding on the ceiling and drawings of ancient Rome on the walls.

Our waiter, neatly dressed in black vest and pants,
cuts fresh bread for us from a large, round loaf. Moments later, he serves our *Castelli Romani*, a dry white
wine with a crisp aftertaste.

The menu is unlike any we've seen so far, devoid of
the usual *tortellini* and *lasagne*. In their place are unique
meat dishes, known only to this area. Slaughter houses
used to surround Testaccio, once the center of Rome's
meat industry. Today, only small butchers remain,
providing local *trattorie* with *trippa*, *pajata*, and *coda*.

Kevin tries *rigatoni con pajata*, fat, cylindrical noo-

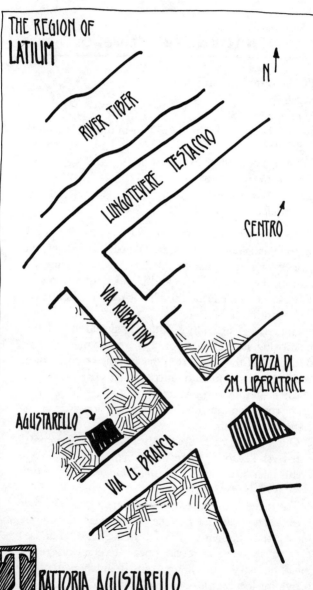

THE REGION OF
LATIUM

N ↑

RIVER TIBER

LUNGOTEVERE TESTACCIO

CENTRO

VIA RUBATTINO

PIAZZA DI
S.M. LIBERATRICE

AGUSTARELLO

VIA G. BRANCA

 TRATTORIA AGUSTARELLO

ROME

dles covered in tomato sauce and slices of lamb intestine. It sounds stranger than it is—the intestines are tender and flavorful. I keep it simple and have *agnolotti casaveca*, savory, meat-filled pasta pockets with a rich tomato/meat sauce—not as intriguing as Kevin's, but just as delicious.

Second course offerings are exotic as well—ox tail, cow's stomach, and more lamb intestines. This time, it's my turn for something a little off-beat. The *trippa alla romana*, cooked for hours in tomato sauce and served with grated *parmigiano* cheese and chopped mint, has a delicate flavor. Kevin enjoys his *involtini al sedano*, thin meat slices rolled with a stuffing of shredded celery and topped with tomato sauce—three distinct flavors blended beautifully.

We congratulate ourselves on finding a vastly different Roman restaurant. Very few eateries in the city offer such interesting fare—a refreshing change from the standard cuts of meat.

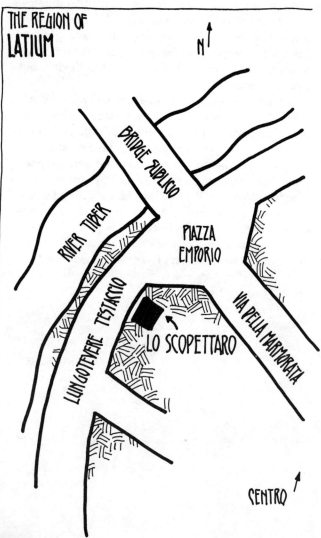

THE REGION OF
LATIUM

N

RIVER TIBER

BRIDGE SUBLICIO

PIAZZA EMPORIO

LUNGOTEVERE TESTACCIO

LO SCOPETTARO

VIA DELLA MARMORATA

CENTRO

RATTORIA LO SCOPETTARO

ROME

Trattoria Lo Scopettaro

Lungotevere Testaccio, 7
Rome
Phone: 574-2408
Hours: noon-3:00pm, 7:00pm-11:30pm. Closed
Tuesday.
Cover charge: 1,500 lire/person. No service charge.
Cost of our meal: 41,000 lire
Not wheel chair negotiable.

Located directly across the Tiber in southern Rome,
Trattoria Lo Scopettaro is steeped in "old world" charm,
housed in a 500-year-old building that's comfortable
and inviting. The entrance is choked by a table of tempting desserts and bowls of fruit and olives.

Kevin and I are led downstairs to the "tavern," a converted wine cellar with a low ceiling and Etruscan
scenes. Wine bottles three-deep line the shelves.

Since this is our final day in Rome, we decide to try
the last of the Roman specialties on our list—*fettuccine
alla romana*, long, flat noodles in a complex sauce of
herbs, tomatoes, mushrooms, white wine, and giblets.
It's served to us steaming hot, with a dollop of sweet
butter and plenty of grated *parmigiano* cheese.

The dining room quickly fills to capacity. Years ago,
this *trattoria*, located in the center of the city's meat industry, was brimming with white-smocked butchers.
But today, long after the slaughter houses have disap-
peared, Lo Scopettaro is stocked with well-dressed business people eager to sample the cuisine that made this
area famous.

As we wipe our plate clean with fresh bread, the
chef/owner walks through the tavern, spending a moment with each of his customers. *"Tutto bene?"* he asks,

smiling. We nod and return the smile. Before he returns to the kitchen, he refills our carafe with *Frascati*.

For my second dish, I have *carne in sugo*, tender chunks of beef with a smooth tomato sauce and thick slices of fleshy mushrooms. Kevin, curious about a food the butchers love to eat, orders *pajata*, a bowl of lamb intestines simmered in tomato sauce. It may sound weird, but according to Kevin, it's tasty and tender. These less-appreciated cuts of meat, called *"alla vaccina"* are found only in *trattorie* surrounding Testaccio and are considered a delicacy by many who grew up there.

Lo Scopettaro's *insalata mista* (mixed salad) is a meal in itself. The large portion of exotic greens, olives, cucumbers, and bits of cheese is a smashing finale to this fabulous, educational feast.

Trattoria Primula

Via Salaria, 146
Rieti
Phone: 73-225
Hours: noon-3:00pm, 7:00pm-10:30pm. Closed
   Tuesday.
Cover charge: 1,500 lire/person. No service charge.
Cost of our meal: 40,000 lire
Wheel chair negotiable. ♿

Driving through a thickly forested valley on a day trip
from Rome, we found Trattoria Primula, three miles
south of the hilltown Rieti. The row of small, stone
houses looks like a truck stop, and, in fact, as we park
the car for lunch, a "big rig" pulls up.

Six tables crowd the little dining room. Black velvet
paintings hang on bright yellow walls with last year's
Christmas decorations. A small space heater stands in
the center of the room, warming away the morning chill.

As we sit down, ready to pour our first glasses of
wine—*Cerveteri*, deep yellow with a lively, dry
flavor—the front door bursts open. A young woman,
cheeks flushed from the cold, is carrying a bucket filled
with just-picked mushrooms. She heads straight for the
kitchen.

My curiosity now piqued, I start with *fusilli con funghi*. The long strands of spiraled spaghetti, chunks of
ham, and chopped mushrooms in tomato sauce is perfect. Kevin selects *ravioli con spinaci*. Their irregular
shapes prove these pasta pockets, stuffed with leafy
spinach and *ricotta* cheese, are made in Primula's kitch-
en. Kevin marvels at the fresh flavor and delicious tomato sauce.

The roar of the traffic on the highway rattles the *trat-*

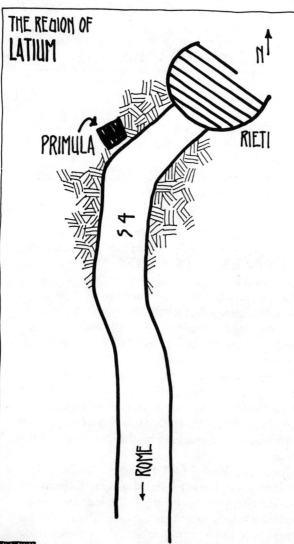

THE REGION OF
LATIUM

N↑

PRIMULA

RIETI

54

← ROME

RATTORIA PRIMULA

RIETI

toria's windows, and more truckers arrive. One by one, they march into the restroom before ordering their lunch.

For seconds, Kevin and I both try one of Latium's favorite meat specialties—*saltimbocca*, thin veal fillets layered with *prosciutto* ham and sage leaves, quickly sautéed in butter and white wine. The herb is an unusual, but perfect, touch.

For dessert, we share a chunk of *caciotta*, young cheese produced locally, and a bowl of fresh figs. After peeling the skin off the fruit, I open it and make a mini-sandwich, with a piece of cheese in the middle. The combination is irresistible.

Some of Latium's best ingredients come from its countryside, and Trattoria Primula has some of the freshest.

THE REGION OF
LATIUM

N ↑

← FRASCATI

VIA IV NOV.

PIAZZA
A. DE
GASPERI

MARINO →

VIA ROMA

CORSO DEL POPOLO

FURLANI
UMBERTO

VIA GARIBALDI

FURLANI UMBERTO

GROTTAFERRATA

Furlani Umberto

Corso del Popolo, 29
Grottaferrata
Phone: 945-9003
Hours: noon-3:00pm, 7:00pm-11:00pm. Closed
  Monday.
Cover charge: 1,000 lire/person.
Service charge: 10%.
Cost of our meal: 42,000 lire
Not wheel chair negotiable.

After a morning of exploring the country outside Rome, Kevin and I stop for lunch at Furlani Umberto in the suburb of Grottaferrata, two miles south of the wine-producing city of Frascati.

As we enter the below-street-level dining area, we're greeted by a fat, gray cat. Twelve paper-covered tables with benches are scattered throughout the panelled room. Resting on the front counter are large jars of olives and artichokes, and an empty fish tank.

The lone diner turns toward us. "Bologna?" he asks, trying to guess where we're from.

"No, we're Americans," Kevin answers in Italian.

"Ah, America. Very good, America," he whispers to himself. Then, as if the conversation never took place, the man returns to his pasta.

A barrel of wine lodged in the wall contains Furlani Umberto's personal stock. Our waitress fills a carafe of the rich, dry wine with a hint of bitter aftertaste.

Tagliolini in brodo is my choice for a first course. The short, thin noodles in savory chicken broth combine for a satisfying treat on this crisp autumn afternoon. Kevin, my pasta-maniac husband, orders *fettuccine a mano*, long, wide noodles made by hand. To top them, he picks *pomodoro*—fresh, chunky tomatoes.

The portly cat continues to roam under every table, covertly receiving or stealing scraps. Be forewarned: if you invite him to sit on your lap, he'll never leave.

We take our cue for the next course from the customers around us and order *bollito con peperoni*. The dish, overflowing with stewed meat and sliced green peppers and onions, is so tender and sweet, we have no trouble finishing every drop, much to the disappointment of the furry friend in my lap. But by the time we leave, he's on the prowl again, and so are we, searching for more great *trattorie* like Furlani Umberto.

Trattoria Camilloni Remo

Via Dello Stadio, 189
Sacrofano
Phone: 908-6059
Hours: 12:30pm-3:00pm, 7:00pm-11:00pm. Closed
    Tuesday.
Cover charge: 2,000 lire/person. No service charge.
Cost of our meal: 58,500 lire
Wheel chair negotiable. &

Not far from Rome, in Latium's horse country, is Trattoria Camilloni Remo, an Italian steakhouse atop a hill.

The dining room is huge, like one in a grand hotel, with broad, stately columns, a 20-foot ceiling, and more than two dozen tables. Along the back wall are old, white refrigerators, filled with slabs of beef. But the focal point of this palatial *trattoria* is a big, brick fireplace.

From our seats, we watch an elderly man clad in a white chef's uniform, cigarette dangling from his mouth, tend to the fire with a long, iron pole. Antonio has been Camilloni Remo's fire master for over two decades. He skillfully moves burning embers from a starter fire to a grill where the meat is cooked. Another man assists him by adding wood and making *bruschetta* (garlic bread).

We immediately order a basket of the olive oil/garlic-smeared toast and a carafe of the house wine, a no-name fermented juice made by the owners, with a light, smooth taste and translucent color.

To begin our meal, Kevin and I try *gnocchi alla romana*. These golden, pancake-shaped dumplings are made from semolina flour, baked until slightly brown, and lavishly served with lots of melted, sweet butter and grated *parmigiano* cheese.

THE REGION OF
LATIUM

N ↑

SACROFANO

CAMILLONI REMO

VIA DELLO STADIO

SACROFANO 7.5 Km.

53

ROME →

 TRATTORIA CAMILLONI REMO

SACROFANO

Once we finish every morsel, we turn our eyes toward the meat team about to prepare the next course. The first man peruses a platter piled high with meat until he finds the perfect cut. After slicing it with a two-foot-long knife, he hands the two-pound sirloin to the fire master, who slaps it on the scalding grid. A few moments later, our waiter delivers the sizzling steak to our table. With just a squeeze of lemon, it melts in our mouths.

There's only one vegetable to have with such a rich specialty—*insalata verde*, a tossed green salad. This one is an interesting mixture of dandelion leaves and watercress.

Though Trattoria Camilloni Remo serves only grilled meats, the variety is enormous, and you could spend a month sampling the various offerings of beef, pork, veal, chicken, and sausage.

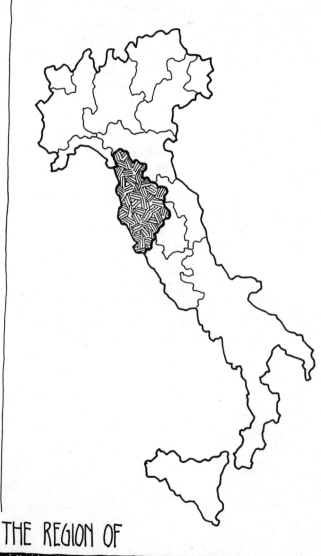

THE REGION OF

USCANY

The Region of Tuscany

Rather than preparing their food in heavy sauces, Tuscans thrive on the natural flavor of grilled meat and poultry. Evidence of Tuscany's simple culinary style is easy to verify. Just follow fragrant smoke down any side street in the region, and you'll find the front doors of *girarrosti*—turnspits, or what Americans call "barbecue/fast-food stands." They nearly outnumber churches.

Visiting a *girarrosto* is a theatrical production to be savored. The show begins at noon, when hungry and hurried office workers crowd the tiny shops. Patrons shout their orders over the sound of chickens, ducks, and other skewered game sizzling above huge fire pits. The cook, clad in a white uniform, stands guard, occasionally stoking the fire. When the meat turns crispy and golden brown, he lifts it off the barbecue with a long pole and slaps it onto a sheet of paper. The cashier quickly wraps the food and hands it to waiting customers. Most only make it a few steps outside before ripping off the paper and biting into the tender, juicy meat.

Unlike *girarrosti*, Tuscany's *trattorie* offer a wide selection of barbecue foods, like *bistecca alla fiorentina* (steak florentine), one of Florence's best-loved specialties. To a typical diner, the recipe seems easy: salt and pepper before grilling, and brush on a little olive oil prior to serving. But what you may not realize is all the decision-making beforehand. Tuscan chefs work only with the finest raw materials. The meat for *bistecca alla fiorentina* is a T-bone steak of a specific thickness. Birch wood is used in the fire for a strong flavor, and the oil is always fresh, extra-virgin from Tuscany's finest olives.

Tuscans don't live by meat alone—beans are the most popular vegetable in this region. In fact, beans appear on the dinner table as appetizers, soups, and side dishes, like *fagioli nel fiasco* (beans in a flask). Italians still use the same time-consuming procedure of cooking the beans in a clear, liter-size bottle over smoldering coals. And most recipes require *cannellini* beans—small, white, and oval-shaped. In spring, peas come into season, bringing forth such delectable Tuscan specialties as *piselli al prosciutto*, peas with ham.

Some say Tuscany was baptized in wine. Its *Chianti*, packaged in the familiar straw-covered bottle, is known around the world. If you purchase a bottle from a Tuscan merchant, he'll require a few hundred lire deposit to guarantee the return of his pear-shaped glass artwork.

Whether it's high in the hills, in a suburban park, on a city rooftop, or in a crowded *trattoria*, Tuscans love to prepare and eat barbecue food. You'll love it, too.

Trattoria l'Cche Ce Ce

Via Magalotti, 11
Florence
Phone: 216-589
Hours: noon-2:30pm, 8:00pm-11:30pm. Closed
  Monday.
Cover charge: 2,000 lire/person. No service charge.
Cost of our meal: 41,500 lire
Wheel chair negotiable. &

Down a narrow alley south of the Duomo, Trattoria
l'Cche Ce Ce offers a warmly lit room filled with framed
posters of paintings by Picasso, Van Gogh, and Gau-
guin. When we arrive in early evening, the chef is standing behind the front counter piled with plates of fresh,
uncooked pasta. He's greeting customers before the full-
blown dinner rush begins.

We sit at the long, communal table in the center of
the room. The booths along the perimeter are for diners
with reservations. For the price of a phone call, they
get the special treatment: two wine glasses instead of
one, and cloth, rather than paper, napkins. But to com-
pensate, the center table is in full view of the dining
room, making it a great spot for people-watching.

Moments after our pasta arrives, the waiter places
a chunk of *parmigiano* cheese and a grater on the table. I use it lavishly all over my *ravioli rose*, large pockets of pasta filled with cheese and topped with a light
tomato/cream sauce. Kevin waits patiently for his turn
to grate the tangy cheese on his *penne strascicate*, hollow pasta cylinders in an olive oil and garlic base, tossed
with chopped turnip greens and *porcini* mushrooms.
Both dishes are elegant!

Sipping *Carmignano*, a vivid red with the scent of

THE REGION OF
TUSCANY

N ↑

PIAZZA
SAN FIRENZE

BORGO DE' GRECI

VIA DEI LEONI

VIA MAGALOTTI

I'CCHE C'È C'È

Trattoria I'cche c'è c'è

FLORENCE

violets, yet mellow and dry, Kevin and I feel like we're at a United Nations conference. On one side are two well-dressed Italian men, smelling of perfume, and on the other, a Japanese couple rummaging through a Berlitz phrase book. We all smile and nod as we watch plates of tempting food pass by.

We do attract our neighbors' attention when the second course arrives. I have *pollastrino alla griglia*, a large, skinned chicken breast, quickly pan-fried, searing in all the juices. Kevin's *coniglio ripieno*, a rabbit fillet rolled with fresh herbs and a hard-boiled egg inside, roasted and sliced, is imaginative and richly flavored.

I'Cche Ce Ce, impossible to pronounce, is equally impossible to forget.

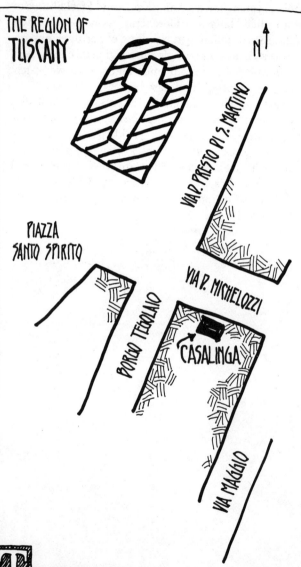

THE REGION OF
TUSCANY

N↑

VIA P. PRESTO DI S. MARTINO

PIAZZA
SANTO SPIRITO

VIA P. MICHELOZZI

BORGO TEGOLAIO

CASALINGA

VIA MAGGIO

TRATTORIA CASALINGA

FLORENCE

Trattoria Casalinga

Via dei Michelozzi, 9
Florence
Phone: 218-624
Hours: noon-2:30pm, 7:00pm-9:30pm. Closed
   Saturday and Sunday.
Cover charge: 1,300 lire/person
Service charge: 900 lire/person
Cost of our meal: 29,000 lire
Wheel chair negotiable. &

Located near the Piazza San Spirito south of the Arno
River, Trattoria Casalinga offers one of the best culinary deals in Florence. The place is sprawling—two
large dining rooms, set in a Renaissance building. Unfortunately, the eatery lost most of its Renaissance ap-
peal during renovations. Twentieth-century pine panels
line the walls, and plaster covers the once-beautiful
cross-ribbed ceiling. But what Casalinga lacks in de-
sign, it amply makes up for in good, regional cooking
at bargain prices.

We skip the *Chianti* tonight and opt for another
variety of Tuscan grape, *Montescudaio*, light, yellow,
with a delicately dry flavor. The wine, coupled with a
basket of fresh bread and rolls, makes us think we're
in the right place.

Ignoring the regular menu, we choose our dinner
from the *piatti del giorno*, the "dishes of the day." I begin with *ravioli alla panna*, small, round pasta enve-
lopes stuffed with *ricotta* cheese, then topped with
cheese/cream and chopped ham sauce. Kevin's *pappardelle al coniglio*, wide ribbon noodles in a tomato-
based rabbit sauce, is a tasty, robust favorite of the
Florentines.

Tonight, like every night, Trattoria Casalinga is crowded. Everyone from starving students and artists to international tourists pack the room or press their noses against the glass, ready to pounce on the next vacant table.

Feeling the pressure to eat and run, Kevin and I proceed to our next course. Kevin picks *faraone arrosto*, a succulent, roasted guinea hen. Between mouthfuls, he declares that the taste is similar to chicken, only better. I try a popular Tuscan specialty, *trippa alla fiorentina*, slowly braised tripe and minced beef, with tomato sauce, herbs, and plenty of *parmigiano* cheese.

After dinner, we walk a block to the Piazza San Spirito, where a concert is underway. The sounds of Mozart provide a wonderful dessert as we sit with our backs against the massive cathedral.

Trattoria Za-Za

Piazza Mercato Centrale, 26
Florence
Phone: 215-411
Hours: noon-2:30pm, 7:00pm-10:30pm. Closed
  Sunday.
No cover charge. No service charge.
Cost of our meal: 43,000 lire
Wheel chair negotiable. &

One afternoon while meandering through the Mercato
Centrale—a collection of outdoor souvenir stands north
of the city—we stumble upon Trattoria Za-Za. Less dat-
ed than other *trattorie* we've discovered, Za-Za has a
distinct Bohemian atmosphere, with rows of *Chianti*
bottles and huge garlic bunches decorating the elaborate
deli counter.

The dining room contains long picnic tables, dressed
with beat-up napkin containers and plastic ashtrays. On
the panelled walls are photographs of celebrity diners,
but I don't recognize the faces. They must be Italian
movie stars.

A waitress approaches our table, singing along with
Madonna's "Like a Virgin" playing in the background.
The young woman slaps a torn piece of brown paper
on our table and places a chunk of thick, crusty bread
on top.

We love our first course of *tris di minestre*, a delicious
collection of three soups served in a compartmental-
ized dish—*ribollita*, made with bread and cabbage, *pap-
pa al pomodoro*, tomato soup, and *passato di fagioli
con farro*, bean purée. To complement this rich specialty
is Tuscany's favorite wine, *Chianti*, the light, dry, red
liquid seen on every table.

THE REGION OF
TUSCANY

N

VIA ROSINA

ZA-ZA

PIAZZA
DEL MERCATO
CENTRALE

VIA SANT' ANTONINO

CENTRO

BORGO LA NOCE

TRATTORIA ZA-ZA

FLORENCE

Za-Za's group dining has customers eating elbow-to-elbow with strangers, but it takes only moments to strike up a conversation with our nearest dinner companion, an actor from London. He tells us he's performing in Florence for the first time. Although I'm interested in his story, I'm more fascinated with the food he's eating: *tagliatelle alle noci*, broad noodles in a walnut and pine nut sauce.

Before embarrassing myself by reaching at his plate to sample this masterpiece, my own entrée arrives—*scaloppine alla livornese*. The thin veal fillets, simmered in wine, tomatoes, garlic, and herbs, are delectable enough to keep me occupied. But, just so I don't miss anything, I taste Kevin's *petti di pollo alla brace*, a thick chicken breast grilled over an open fire.

Our dessert, *lamponi alla crema di mascarpone*, arrives as the actor is finishing. While swallowing his last strand of *tagliatelle*, he tells us he's appearing in "A Midsummer Night's Dream." My mouth is watering, and I ask, "But what about your pasta?" He smiles, slowly wiping his plate with a piece of bread, and says, "It was delicious."

So were our fresh raspberries and sweet, creamy cheese custard, an angelic finish to this heavenly dinner.

THE REGION OF
TUSCANY

N ↑

BORGO DEGLI ALBIZI

PIAZZA
G. SALVEMINI

OSTERIA

VIA M. PALMIERI

← CENTRO

VIA GHIBELLINA

STERIA

FLORENCE

Osteria

Via Parimieri, 37
Florence
No phone.
Hours: 12:30pm-3:00pm, 7:00pm-11:00pm. Closed
   Tuesday.
Cost of our meal: 13,000 lire each (fixed price)
Wheel chair negotiable. &

Although this tiny *trattoria* in the center of Florence
doesn't have an indoor dining area, it offers the best
deal in town for good, local food.

Kevin and I examine the hand-printed menu posted
on the door of the kitchen, an annexed room of a large,
stone tower. For just 13,000 lire, the chef serves two
courses—pasta and meat—plus salad and wine. Usually, we avoid fixed priced menus because of their
unimaginative offerings, but we had a hunch Osteria
would be different. Plus, the price is unbeatable, so we
take a seat on the umbrella-covered platform. The other
five tables are filled. Obviously, the word is out.

A waitress delivers a half-carafe of *Pisano*, a palatable white wine with a slightly bitter aftertaste, and a
basket of warm, crusty bread. We nibble and sip the
wine while watching hurried lunch-time pedestrians.

Then the pasta arrives. My *fusilli tricolore ricotta*,
three types of curly noodles—carrot, spinach, and
semolina—covered in a basic *ricotta* cheese sauce, is
beautiful to look at, as well as tasty. Kevin's *spaghetti
alla ciugata*, pasta with an anchovy purée, is also uncomplicated, but perfect for my fish-loving husband.

For our second course, I try a favorite grilled
specialty—*bistecche di maiale*, a large pork chop cooked
to order and served sizzling hot and juicy. When I'm

sure no one is looking, I pick up the meaty bone and gnaw off the meat closest to the bone—it's always the sweetest. Something this good shouldn't go to waste.

Kevin laughs at my questionable manners, but understands completely. His *pollo fritto*, Tuscan fried chicken, is cause for finger-licking, too. Prepared differently than most, this recipe requires the chicken to marinate in lemon juice and olive oil before it's batter-dipped and deep-fried.

After lunch, we head down the street for a pastry, since Osteria doesn't offer dessert. We don't mind, though. With a deal like that, we can afford to have *gelati*, too.

Trattoria Quattro Leoni

Via dei Vellutini, 1
Florence
Phone: 218-562
Hours: noon-2:30pm, 7:00pm-9:30 pm. Closed
   Saturday evening and all day Sunday.
Cover charge: 1,500 lire/person. No service charge.
Cost of our meal: 31,500 lire
Wheel chair negotiable. &

Located south of the Arno River on a small, residential
piazza, Trattoria Quattro Leoni has barely changed over
the past 20 years. Three connecting dining rooms, lined
with worn, wood wainscoting, feel as comfortable as
a pair of faded jeans. Modest tablecloths and plastic
bread baskets, dating to the 1950's, grace every table.
Since Quattro Leoni can't rely on its good looks for customers, it woos folks with delicious, inexpensive food.

Steam from the kitchen coats the dining room windows. As the *signora* prepares our first course, her
apron-clad husband silently scrubs pots.

Pappardelle alla lepre, wide ribbon noodles with rabbit sauce, is a favorite Tuscan specialty because the people of this region love to hunt, and they fill their kitchens
with small game. The dish we're enjoying is a hearty
combination of meat, tomatoes, red wine, fresh herbs,
and juniper berries. Highlighting the meal is a carafe
of *Carmignano*, a lively, dry red wine with the scent
of violets.

For our second course, we again follow the suggestion of our waiter and order the evening special. Kevin
has *pollo alla cacciatora*, plump pieces of chicken simmered in a savory tomato sauce. I pick *capponcello arrosto*, breast of capon roasted with butter and herbs.

THE REGION OF
TUSCANY

RIVER ARNO

N↑

BORGO SAN JACOPO

VIA DEI VELLUTINI

QUATTRO LEONI

VIA TOSCANELLA

CENTRO ↑

PIAZZA DE' PITTI

TRATTORIA QUATTRO LEONI

FLORENCE

Rounding out our meal is a bowl of *fagioli lessi* (white beans). They arrive at our table plain, ready to be dressed in a drizzle of olive oil and a dash of pepper—another Tuscan favorite, and quickly becoming one of ours.

After dinner, we pause in the *piazza*, and reflect on the satisfying simplicity of Quattro Leoni. All in all, we're glad it hasn't changed.

THE REGION OF
TUSCANY

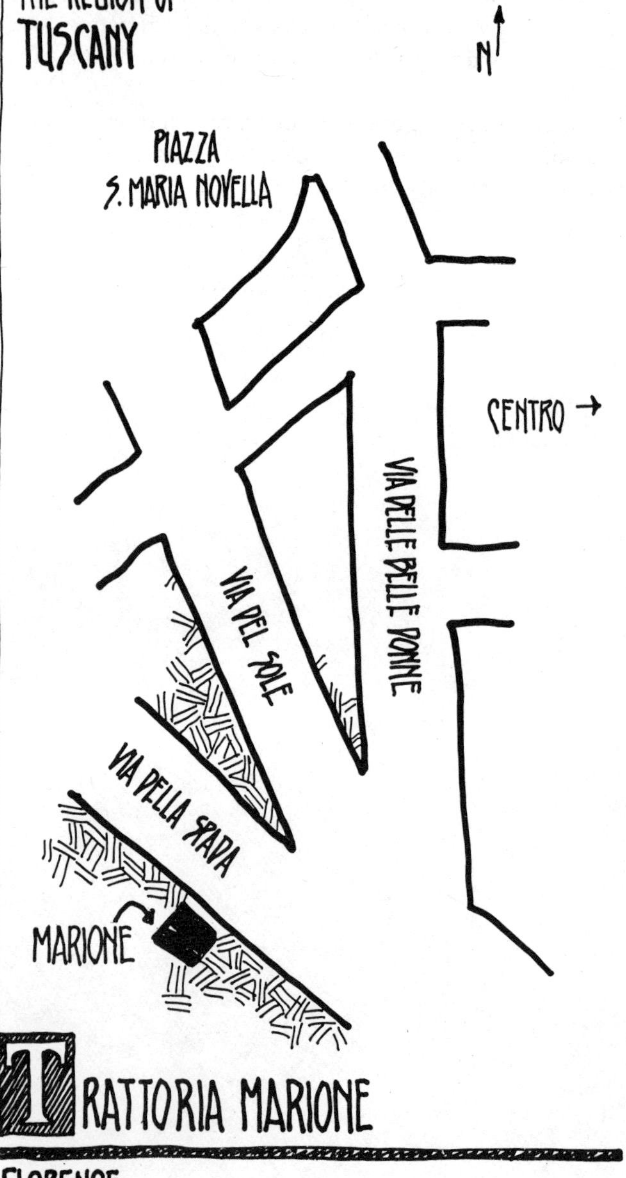

TRATTORIA MARIONE

FLORENCE

Trattoria Marione

Via della Spada, 27
Florence
Phone: 214-756
Hours: noon-2:30pm, 7:00pm-10:30pm. Closed
   Saturday and Sunday.
Cover charge: 1,300 lire/person
Service charge: 10%
Cost of our meal: 36,500 lire
Wheel chair negotiable. ♿

Trattoria Marione is my pick for the best dining spot
in Florence. Located north of the Arno River and west
of the city center, Marione is loud and active. Two dozen
tables crowd three, small dining rooms. The ceiling is
made of dark wood and an intricate, inlaid square pat-
tern. Unfortunately, it's marred by funky fluorescent
lights. Behind the front deli counter is a shelf stocked
with dusty wine bottles dating to the 19th century.

   Like everyone else in the restaurant, we order a carafe
of the only wine Marione offers—*Chianti*. Luckily,
Kevin and I haven't tired of this lusciously light, dry
red wine.

   Marione lovingly concocts a new, extensive menu
every day. I start with *ribollita con l'olio di frantoio*,
which translated means "reboiled." The morning after
this soup is made, it's cooked again, making it so thick
it's almost a stew. The combination of cabbage, beans,
and bread in savory vegetable stock is a harmony of
distinct flavors. I follow the way other Italians eat *ribollita* and pour a generous amount of *olio* (olive oil) on
top.

   Kevin sticks with one of his favorites—*pasta corta
alla boscaiola*, long noodles in a simple sauce of *porcini* mushrooms, olive oil, and chopped parsley.

Thinking nothing can taste any better, our second plates actually rival the first, starting with my *stracotto con melanzane*. These thin strips of beef, simmered in a zesty tomato sauce for several hours, are fork-tender. The sautéed eggplant side dish is sweet and garlicky. Kevin is amazed at the size and wonderful taste of his *trota alla griglia*, a two-pound fresh trout stuffed with long stalks of rosemary and grilled to perfection.

The friendly service, low prices, and marvelous regional dishes make Trattoria Marione worth visiting as often as possible.

Trattoria Da Ginone

Via dei Serragli, 35
Florence
Phone: 218-758
Hours: noon-2:30pm, 7:00pm-10:00pm. Closed
   Sunday.
Cover charge: 1,500 lire/person. No service charge.
Cost of our meal: 26,000 lire
Wheel chair negotiable. &

This busy little *trattoria*, south of the Arno River, is set up differently than most. Several pasta and meat dishes are prepared each day and then served swiftly from a cafeteria-style console. The menu steers away from things that need to be cooked to order, like spaghetti, and concentrates on items like soups, stews, and lasagna.

The atmosphere is casual. Tables and chairs made of polished pine are scattered through a room decorated with old photos of Florence. There's even sawdust coating the floor.

Pinned on one wall is a hand-written sign on a white placemat: "*Venerdì* (Friday), *CACCIUCCO*." This spicy fish soup, made with lobster, shrimp, mussels, clams, and any other available fish, lots of vegetables, red chili peppers, and croutons, is a favorite among the natives.

We start with *riso di fagioli*, a savory soup of rice in a thick golden, chickpea bean purée. Like the Tuscans, we never tire of trying the different styles of bean soup. Trattoria Da Ginone's wine is *Chianti*, with that familiar ruby color and smooth, dry flavor. Although it's easy to drink a lot of it, we limit ourselves to a half-liter.

Da Ginone's next offerings are varied and innovative.

THE REGION OF
TUSCANY

N ↑

RIVER
ARNO

LUNGARNO GUICCIARDINI

VIA DE' SERRAGLI

VIA S. AGOSTINO

CENTRO ↗

DA GINONE

TRATTORIA DA GINONE

FLORENCE

I try *petto di pollo al prosciutto,* a moist, skinned chicken breast covered with melted *mozzarella* cheese and thinly sliced ham. Kevin's *braciola arrostolata,* pork loin rolled with herbs and a hard-boiled egg, then roasted, is a delicious recipe. We also have an order of *carote,* fresh carrots cooked with a bit of butter.

For the quickest service and great, inexpensive Tuscan specialties anytime of the day, Da Ginone's can't be beat.

THE REGION OF
TUSCANY

N↑

VIA DELLA SAPIENZA

VIA DELLE TERME

LA CELLINA

VIA S. CATERINA

PIAZZA
DEL CAMPO

RATTORIA LA CELLINA

SIENA

Trattoria La Cellina

Via delle Terme, 52
Siena
Phone: 283-133
Hours: noon-2:30pm, 7:00pm-11:00pm. Closed
  Sunday.
Cover charge: 1,500 lire/person
Service charge: 15%
Cost of our meal: 43,500 lire
Wheel chair negotiable. ♿

It's raining when we arrive in Siena, the medieval walled
city in the center of Tuscany. The main *piazza*, Il
Campo—where the annual horse race *Il Palio* is held—
surges with umbrellas and yellow rain slickers. "A day
like this is meant to be spent indoors, eating," I tell
Kevin. So we forego touring the giant clock tower and
instead slip down narrow stone passageways toward
Trattoria La Cellina.

The warm interior is a welcome retreat, and we hang
our wet coats on a large, wooden rack. Blue Florentine
tile and ceramic plates hang from the walls. On every
table, Tuscan wine bottles await inspection and consumption. We order the house wine. The room-tem-
perature *Chianti* is warming as it goes down.

I start with *pastina in brodo*, crumb-size pasta in a
rich chicken broth. With a piece of bread in one hand,
I'm ready to begin. Kevin has something heartier—
penne alla boscaiola, long, tubular noodles in a thick
tomato and mushroom sauce. Both dishes are superb.

From the kitchen, the grilling Tuscan meat issues an
intoxicating aroma and musical sizzle, luring more people into La Cellina. We can't resist the temptation, either.
Kevin tries the *calamari alla griglia* (grilled squid). He

loves the simplicity of this seafood and adds just a squeeze of lemon. My *fettina di vitello alla griglia*, small slices of grilled veal without sauce, is flavorful and tender.

Feeling amply fortified, we venture back into the rain and spend the rest of the afternoon exploring Siena, a well-preserved Renaissance jewel.

Trattoria La Buca

Corso Il Rossellino, 38
Pienza
Phone: 748-448
Hours: noon-2:30pm, 7:00pm-10:00pm. Closed
   Monday.
Cover charge: 2,000 lire/person. No service charge.
Cost of our meal: 50,000 lire
Wheel chair negotiable. ♿

Trattoria La Buca, beautifully designed, wins my vote
for one of the best *trattorie* in northern Italy. Located
in the hilltown of Pienza, which was settled over 500
years ago, this eatery makes us feel like we're dining in
a royal castle. Although renovated to accommodate a
modern kitchen, the dining room retains a palatial
mood. Large, crumbling stone columns shoulder exposed brick archways. The cross-ribbed ceiling is as high
as a cathedral's, and "old world" details abound, from
primitive lanterns to wrought iron, padlocked gates.

To start this banquet in proper style, we order *No-
bile Pantano*, the local red wine with a pungent, dry
flavor. For our first course, the waitress suggests Kevin
try the house specialty, *pici della casa*, a fat, spaghetti-
type pasta in spicy meat sauce. It's heavy, but delicious.
I indulge in *zuppa di pane* (bread soup). The unusual
but tasty combination of thick, crusty bread in a tomato
base is simple, hilltown fare.

"Try the turkey," whispers our waitress. "It's very
fresh." The *petto di tacchino*, thick slices of turkey breast
in its own savory juice, is indeed wonderful and a trib-
ute to Tuscany's talent for roasting fowl.

Although we're full, we're presented with the dessert
cart and my favorite after-dinner treat—*tiramisù*. Trans-

THE REGION OF
TUSCANY

MONTEPULCIANO →

N ↑

VAL ENZO MANGIA VACCHI

PIAZZA
DANTE ALIGHIERI

CORSO IL ROSSELLINO

PIAZZA
PIO II

← LA BUCA

TRATTORIA LA BUCA

PIENZA

lated, it means, "Pick me up." The recipe starts with sponge cake soaked in *vin santo*, or Marsala wine, then layered with a fluffy *mascarpone* cheese and cream mousse, and topped with a generous dusting of cocoa powder. It's so scrumptious I could eat two, but I resist the temptation.

From the bottom of the cart, our waitress pulls out an unmarked bottle and motions for our glasses. She fills them half-way with a strong-smelling, orange liquid.

"*Vin santo*?" I ask.

"Yes," she answers proudly. "It's our own, made here in town." The sweet, Italian dessert wine is a perfect addition to the afternoon.

Kevin and I linger at La Buca's for another hour, content as well-fed royalty of long-ago. And when the bill arrives, it's a mere pittance, well within the commoners' budget.

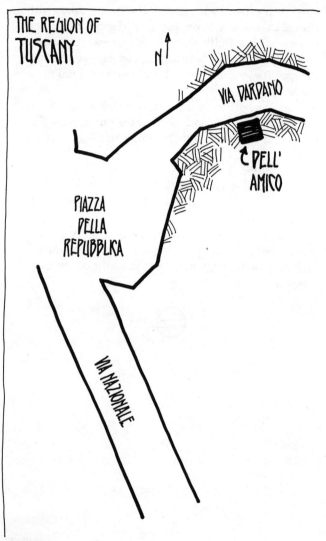

THE REGION OF
TUSCANY

N

VIA DARDANO

C. DELL'
AMICO

PIAZZA
DELLA
REPUBBLICA

VIA NAZIONALE

RATTORIA DELL' AMICO

CORTONA

Trattoria Dell'Amico

Via Dardano, 12
Cortona
Phone: 604-192
Hours: noon-2:00pm, 6:30pm-10:00pm. Closed
  Monday.
Cover charge: 1,500 lire/person. No service charge.
Cost of our meal: 35,500 lire
Wheel chair negotiable. &

Steeped in Etruscan history, the ancient, walled city of
Cortona stands 2,000 feet above sea level. The town was
constructed on southern slopes covered in olive groves
and overlooking the valley near Lake Trasimeno.

The noon church bell announces our arrival, as Kevin
and I climb the flagstone passageways to reach Trattoria Dell'Amico. Outside, there's a handwritten menu
with cut-out pictures of the food—a tempting display
of pastas and soups. The dining room has six long tables, each dressed in blue plaid cloth. Souvenirs from
around the world—a silk fan, a pair of castanets, a German flag—surround a disorganized front bar overflowing with jars of olives and wheels of *pecorino*
cheese.

Carrying a carafe of *Valdichiana*, a straw-yellow wine
with a buttery, dry taste, the smiling *signora* approaches
our table. She tells us about the day's special, *penne
al gorgonzola*, long, tubular noodles smothered in a
creamy, biting cheese sauce. It's Kevin's favorite, and
I wholeheartedly agree. Extra chunks of unmelted
cheese on top please him even more.

Happy that we're enjoying her food, the *signora* goes
behind an old gingham curtain into the kitchen. We hear
her pounding meat and chopping vegetables in prepa-

ration for our next course—an assurance that the meal is fresh and cooked to order.

Kevin's *scaloppine al pizzaiola* (veal fillets), simmered in a spicy tomato sauce and lots of black olives, deserves big raves; and so does my *agnello ai ferri*, grilled lamb rubbed with rosemary and olive oil.

Before we leave town, we take a stroll along the remains of the Etruscan walls, now overgrown and crumbling. Cortona, like many country hilltowns, delights us with her unpretentious *trattoria*.

Trattoria La Curvaccia

Via Chiantigiana, 20 (Route 222)
Le Bolle
Phone: 854-151
Hours: 12:30pm-3:00pm, 7:00pm-10:00pm. Closed
   Wednesday.
Cover charge: 3,500 lire/person. No service charge.
Cost of our meal: 47,000 lire
Wheel chair negotiable. &

Traveling along Route 222, a country road twisting
through Tuscany's Chianti region, Kevin and I stumble
upon Trattoria La Curvaccia. The stone house setting,
complete with tiny general store and a collie sleeping
on the front stoop, is too tempting to pass, so we stop
for lunch.

Inside, we're greeted by the *signora*, a plump, older
woman, her dark hair tightly wound into a bun.
"Chianti?" she asks. We nod in unison. The rich, dry
wine is produced on the premises (additional bottles
are for sale) and is the **only** wine drunk in the area.

La Curvaccia is a homey little place, with only six
tables and colorful ceramic plates decorating the walls.
The fire from the large brick oven in the corner adds
to the warm, comfortable ambiance.

The *signora* returns with our wine, shuffling her
slipper-clad feet across the slate floor. We ignore the
regular menu and take suggestions from our
chef/hostess. "The *minestrone* is fresh. I made it this
morning," she confides.

In moments, she presents two hot bowls of vegetable soup, filled with beans, potatoes, carrots, and pasta. While we soak up the extra broth, tearing off pieces
of warm bread, we watch the *signora* prepare our next

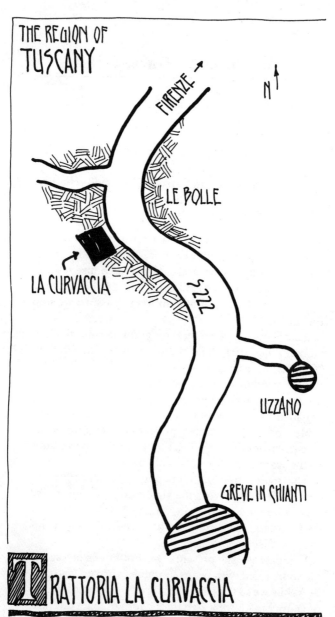

THE REGION OF
TUSCANY

FIRENZE →

N ↑

LE BOLLE

LA CURVACCIA

S 222

UZZANO

GREVE IN CHIANTI

TRATTORIA LA CURVACCIA

LE BOLLE

course, *pollo al forno* (baked chicken). Using a long, iron pole, she concentrates on stoking the fire as she moves the red-hot embers around a pan full of chicken. After 45 minutes, the chicken's ready—brown and juicy, with just a slight smoky flavor and aroma.

After lunch, we take a walk around the farm. Hills rise and fall for miles, and every inch of land is covered with grape vines. Before driving off, we purchase some of La Curvaccia's Chianti, so later, on a special occasion, we can uncork the memory of this special country *trattoria*.

THE REGION OF
TUSCANY

N ↑

FIRENZE →

TAVARNELLE

S2

BARBERINO

LA SOSTA →

SIENA →

TRATTORIA LA SOSTA

BARBERINO

Trattoria La Sosta

Route 2
Barberino Val d'Elsa
Phone: 807-5626
Hours: 12:30pm-3:00pm, 6:30pm-10:30pm. Closed
  Tuesday.
Cover charge: 2,000 lire/person. No service charge.
Cost of our meal: 57,000 lire
Outside (summer only) wheel chair negotiable. ♿

I owe the discovery of Trattoria La Sosta to my sister
Mary Ella and brother-in-law John. While vacationing
in Tuscany, they stumbled upon this country eatery and
fell in love with the place.

"You have to go there Thursday, Saturday, or Sunday," Mary Ella told me. "That's when they fire-up the
outside barbecue for *bistecca fiorentina*—Florentine
steaks. One of the nights we were there, the baby was
being fussy. Just as John was trying to put Cara to sleep,
our steaks arrived. When the owner saw our trouble,
he immediately took them back to the grill and covered
them with a plate to keep them warm. When the baby
fell asleep, he served them hot and juicy."

Just as Mary Ella described, Kevin and I easily find
La Sosta along Route 2, a two-lane country road meandering through Tuscany's Chianti region, a hilly area
speckled with villas, slender cypresses, and neatly furrowed vineyards.

La Sosta has been lovingly transformed from a barn
to a contemporary eatery. Many of the original features
have been left intact, like the stone exterior, brick interior, and even a terra-cotta water trough along the
back wall of the dining room.

As a prelude to the *bistecca*, we have *rigatoni al funghi porcini*, fat pasta tubes tossed with olive oil,

chopped parsley, and meaty *porcini* mushrooms, which grow at the base of chestnut and oak trees after a rain. This irresistible dish is served in a traditional clay pot and enhanced by a carafe of *Chianti*.

Barbecuing is an art in Tuscany, handed down from father to son. Although steak is the most popular meat, veal, sausage, and chicken are also available and often cooked *alla brace*—over charcoal.

Our inch-thick sirloin arrives just the way we like it—slightly charred, but rare inside. No one else grills steak the way Tuscans do.

For dessert, we order *cantucci con vin santo*—crisp, almond-flavored cookies and a shot-glass of sweet Tuscan wine. Like kids after school, we dip the cookies in the wine till soft, then let them melt in our mouths. The liquid burns our throats and clears our noses—it's strong stuff!

The Region of Veneto

Stretching from the massive Dolomite Alps in the north to Venice at the mouth of the Adriatic Sea, the region of Veneto in northeast Italy is an area with spectacular terrain and diverse climates. Its gastronomic heart is Venice, a city bulging with intricate canals and an artist's palette of facades.

During the 13th century, Venice was an enormous port and the gateway to the East for importers like Marco Polo. The early Venetians—skillful artisans and merchants—were highly civilized and quite modern in their lifestyle. The hurried businessmen had no time for elaborate meals, so they sought the finest ingredients—fresh local seafood, rice from Lombardy, cornmeal from Friuli—and developed an uncomplicated cuisine. Today, Venice still attracts international businessmen—but mostly hungry tourists—and those glorious regional specialties live on.

Venetians dip into the nearby Adriatic for their main courses. The most popular, *scampi alla venezia*, large shrimp sauteed in olive oil, lemon juice, and garlic, is known throughout the world. Another favorite is *cape sante*, thick, breaded scallops simmered in white wine and lemon juice.

Like other northern regions, rice rules in Veneto. Unlike their neighbors in Lombardy, who prefer simple rice dishes, Venetians, in keeping with their artistic past, use the rice bowl as a blank canvas and add different ingredients and colors—black rice for *risotto nero*, inkfish for *risotto de seppie*, and small, sweet peas for *risi e bisi*.

THE REGION OF
ENETO

Venetians use a very fine, white maize for their *polenta*. Local mothers say the purest recipe—*polenta e latte*, cornmeal with milk—is so nutritious they give it to just-weaned babies. Spicier versions of this staple include *polenta pasticciata*, baked with tomatoes, herbs, and beef, and *polenta pastizada*, layered with veal and vegetables in a white wine/tomato sauce.

Venetians' favorite vegetable is *radicchio*, grown north of Venice in Treviso. This dark red, slightly bitter lettuce is prepared grilled (*radicchio di treviso*) or with bacon (*radicchio alla pancetta*). Both are served steaming hot, crisp, and drizzled with fresh olive oil.

Like Veneto's diverse environment, regional wines range from the finest in Italy to the simplest table fare. The best are *Bardolino*, a red wine similar to *Chianti*; *Valpolicella*, a rich, red wine; and *Soave*, a light, dry, white wine—all produced around the city of Verona.

Veneto has so much to offer—from the beauty and cuisine of Venice to the Renaissance ruins and furrowed vineyards scattered across the countryside—that you'll find it hard to move on to your next destination.

NOTE: While searching for the *trattorie* we recommend in Venice, please note that the printed addresses **never** match the maps! It's a mystery that only Venetians understand. If you go by the addresses you'll drive yourself crazy, so follow the maps only.

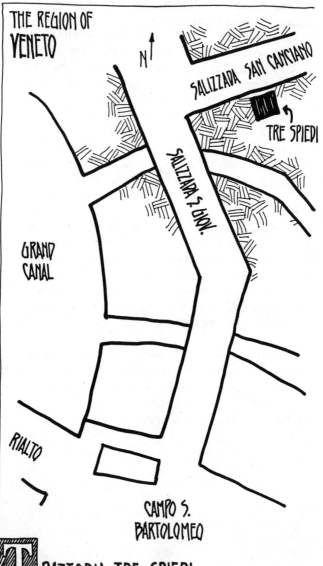

THE REGION OF
VENETO

N

SALIZZADA SAN CANCIANO

TRE SPIEDI

SALIZZADA S. GIOV.

GRAND
CANAL

RIALTO

CAMPO S.
BARTOLOMEO

RATTORIA TRE SPIEDI

VENICE

Trattoria Tre Spiedi

Cannaregio, 5906
Venice
Phone: 520-8035
Hours: noon-2:00pm, 7:00pm-11:30pm. Closed
   Monday.
Cover charge: 2,000 lire/person. No service charge.
Cost of our meal: 53,000 lire
Not wheel chair negotiable.

First the good news: there's plenty of low-priced restaurants in Venice. The bad news: most offer only tourist
menus, a dull mixture of pasta and meat. With this in
mind, Kevin and I start at the tourist mecca San Marco
Square and walk north through the crowded, twisting
streets. When the language in the streets changes from
English and German to Italian, so do the menus.

We discover Trattoria Tre Spiedi on our way back to
the hotel after one of those disappointing, dull, tourist
meals. Pausing at the entrance to listen, I whisper to
Kevin, "Which language are they speaking?"

"Italian," he responds, immediately pulling a map
from his back pocket and marking the location.

On our return the following evening, two rather large
waiters, dressed in white, nautical shirts, greet us at the
door. We follow them past a glass cabinet filled with
all kinds of fresh fish on ice. Patrons peruse the display
and then make their selections.

The dining room is dark and intimate—bare wood,
exposed bricks, beam ceiling, wrought iron lamps, and
a single Doric column. A strange mix of framed pictures hangs on the wall: many are autographed etch-
ings, expressionist in style, drawn on placemats and
pizza boxes.

Skipping the regular menu, we order "the day's specials"—*i piatti del giorno*. For pasta, we try *gnocchi del pesce*, puffy potato dumplings in a mild tomato, cream, and salmon sauce. A half-bottle of the house wine, *Tocai*—white and dry, with a sharp bite—arrives with a basket of crunchy, thick bread. We quickly gobble up both.

Bisato in umido con polenta is our second course selection. Braised eel surrounded by tomato sauce and a dollop of creamy white *polenta*—made from neighboring Friuli's finer maize—is an unusual, but delicious, combination. Tre Spiedi's *insalata mista* (mixed salad) is an interesting montage of fresh dandelion greens, watercress, *radicchio*, and fennel.

Finished, we return to San Marco Square. The restaurants are hopping, the streets are crowded, but there's not an Italian in sight—they're all dining in *trattorie* like Tre Spiedi.

Trattoria Casalinga Dalla Cea

Calle del Fumo, 5422
Venice
Phone: 523-7450
Hours: noon-2:00pm, 7:00pm-10:00pm. Closed
  Sunday.
Cover charge: 1,000 lire/person. No service charge.
Cost of our meal: 41,500 lire
Not wheel chair negotiable.

Kevin and I spot Trattoria Casalinga Dalla Cea beneath
a vine-covered trellis in a small *piazza* near the Grand
Canal. In the front window, perched against wine bottles, is a hand-printed menu offering a variety of regional specialties.

We eagerly enter. A Corinthian column in the center
of the small room balances a low ceiling. Two wine jugs
filled with local *Bardolino* sit on a long front counter,
so we begin with a carafe of the luscious red liquid—
light bouquet, slightly bitter and dry—a favorite in this
region.

Our waiter approaches with a piece of green paper
he just ripped from a roll in the corner and covers our
table with it. At 7:00pm, we're his first customers for
the evening, but it isn't long before the locals arrive for
dinner.

Kevin and I start with *fusilli al tonno e piselli*, curly
pasta noodles tossed in cream sauce, chunks of grilled
fresh tuna, and Veneto's beloved sweet peas.

While we eat, six men dressed in blue uniforms walk
in and yell to the *signora*, busily cooking in the kitch-
en. They operate the *vaporetti*, the canal's water buses.
Three liters of wine are brought to their table, and the
men roll up their sleeves in preparation for pasta.

THE REGION OF
VENETO

N ↑

CASALINGA
DALLA CEA

CALLE D. FUIO BURANELLI

CALLE VARISCO

CALLE D. BONDI

CAMPIELLO
STELLA

↙ GRAND CANAL

↓ SAN MARCO

CAMPIELLO
WIDMAN

CALLE WIDMAN

 TRATTORIA CASALINGA DALLA CEA

VENICE

For my entrée I select another regional favorite—*sarde in saor*, fresh sardines from the Adriatic, deep-fried and marinated in red wine vinegar, onions, pine nuts, and herbs. The fragrant pickling juice captures Kevin's attention, but not for long. *Costicine al vino bianco*, several small veal chops simmered in white wine, requires his full concentration.

Dessert and two cups of Italian coffee follow. *Zabaione con le fragole*, a creamy *vin santo* wine custard and fresh strawberries, is a sweet accompaniment to the strong, rich *espresso*.

We finish the same time the *vaporetti* drivers do and walk behind them as they drunkenly traverse the hushed streets, singing operettas.

THE REGION OF
VENETO

N ↑

← SAN MARCO

VIA GARIBALDI

FONDAMENTA DI S. ANNA

ALLA RAMPA

VIALE GARIBALDI

RATTORIA ALLA RAMPA

VENICE

Trattoria Alla Rampa

Castello, 1135
Venice
Phone: 528-5365
Hours: noon-3:00pm, 7:00pm-10:00pm. Closed
  Sunday.
Cover charge: 1,500 lire/person
Service charge: 10%
Cost of our meal: 40,000 lire
Not wheel chair negotiable.

Determined not to share our table with fellow American tourists, Kevin and I are on the prowl again for an out-of-the-way, Venetian dining spot that only locals know. Today, we investigate establishments on Via Garibaldi, a wide walkway perpendicular to the city's eastern shore, near the Maritime Museum.

We arrive at Garibaldi near noon, just as the daily fruit market is winding down. The shoppers are still out in full force, talking on the street corners, their straw baskets brimming with fresh produce.

On a hunch, Kevin and I follow a group of fish vendors who seem to need liquid refreshment, hoping they'll lead us to a culinary treasure. Sure enough, when they reach the end of the boulevard, they make a bee line for a crowded bar. I squint to read the sign, painted faintly above the narrow doorway: Trattoria Alla Rampa.

"Bingo," I say to Kevin, as we push our way inside. We squeeze past the long deli counter and two enormous jugs of wine, then duck under a staircase to get into the dining area. The room, a converted storage space, has no windows and only six paper-covered tables, but no camera-clad visitors. (Well, maybe two, but we don't count.)

The door to the kitchen is open, exposing a hair-netted *signora* moving quickly from pot to pan. She smiles as we take our seats. Our waitress brings a half-carafe of *Verduzzo*, a white, dry wine made a few miles outside Venice. We relish its snappy taste, anticipating our first bite of Alla Rampa's regional fare.

Kevin's *spaghetti con tonno*, pasta and fresh chunks of albacore tuna with a drizzle of olive oil, is an unusual but delicious blend. I have *spaghetti con carne*, pasta with pieces of braised beef and tomato sauce—wonderful!

No time to back down, Kevin tells me, as he orders our next course. He goes easy on me and orders something light—*fegato alla veneziana*, liver and onions. This precisely executed recipe is the #1 one dish of Venice—and infinitely better than what was served in my school cafeteria. Thin slices of calf's liver are cooked rapidly so they don't dry out. The onions are sautéed separately and then added on top before serving. The result is fantastic.

Only a few stands are open in the outdoor market when we emerge several hours later. That's good because we're so full, we don't want to look at any more food. At least not until dinnertime.

Trattoria Alle Oche

S. Giacomo dell'Orio, 1552
Venice
Phone: 524-1161
Hours: noon-2:00pm, 7:00pm-11:00pm. Closed
   Monday.
Cover charge: 1,000 lire/person
Service charge: 12%
Cost of our meal: 49,000 lire
Not wheel chair negotiable.

While Kevin and I survey the menu posted outside Trattoria Alle Oche, an elderly Italian couple comes through the heavy wooden door into the cool, evening air. They pause to button their coats and praise the dinner they just ate. No need for discussion between us—a local's recommendation is our best indicator.

The inside of this *trattoria* looks surprisingly like an American tavern. Stretching the length of the room, a large mahogany bar faces a row of private, step-up booths with burgundy leather seats. The back room is actually a tent-covered platform where, on hot summer nights, the management rolls back the ceiling for *al frésco* dining. We sit in this makeshift dining hall and order a carafe of wine. The *Valpolicella*, ruby red with a velvety, dry flavor, is a perfect start to our meal.

For his first round, Kevin indulges in *gnocchi al basilico*, bite-size potato dumplings tossed in cream and chopped basil. Although the sauce is similar to *pesto*, Kevin proclaims it smoother, not nearly as tangy, with a purer basil flavor. My *quadruci di carciofi* is a tempting combination of small pasta pockets stuffed with cheese and garnished with artichoke petals in a chopped tomato sauce.

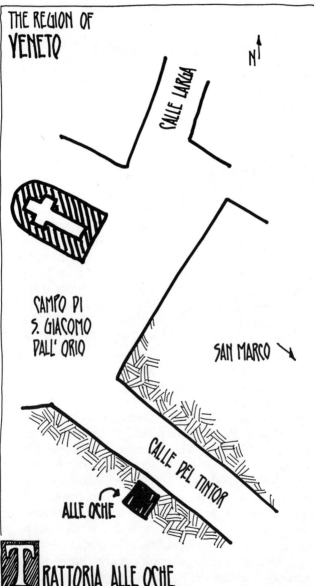

THE REGION OF
VENETO

N↑

CALLE LARGA

CAMPO DI
S. GIACOMO
DALL' ORIO

SAN MARCO ↘

CALLE DEL TINTOR

ALLE OCHE

TRATTORIA ALLE OCHE

VENICE

American rock 'n roll blares over the sound system, and more people pile in. The crowd is a mixture of college students converging on the bar and hungry families working on their second pizzas.

After a brief intermission, our next dishes arrive. My *scampi ai ferri*, large local shrimp marinated in garlic and olive oil then sprinkled with paprika and a squeeze of lemon before grilling, are succulent and flavorful. Kevin has seafood on his mind, too. His *sogliola ai ferri* (grilled sole) comes to him straight off the fire. With a brush of butter and lemon, it's a tasty meal.

After dinner, we take our *passeggiata* (promenade) through the dark Venetian streets, and we decide nighttime is best for discovering Venice. In stark contrast to the day, few people are around, so we feel we have this magnificent city all to ourselves.

THE REGION OF
VENETO

N ↑

CENTRO ↗

VIA CRISTOFORO MORO

ALLA VIGNA

VIA RIVIERA PALEOCAPA

VIA CERNAIA

PIAZZA
PORTA SARACINESSA

VIA P. PAOLI

 RATTORIA ALLA VIGNA

PADUA

Trattoria Alla Vigna

Via Calle Pace, 97
Padua
Phone: 871-9709
Hours: noon-2:00pm, 7:00pm-11:30pm. Closed
  Sunday.
Cover charge: 2,000 lire/person. No service charge.
Cost of our meal: 31,000 lire
Not wheel chair negotiable.

Trattoria Alla Vigna is just inside the southwest entrance
of the walled city of Padua. An illegible, rain-stained
menu hangs outside a battered front door, but looks
are deceiving. Once past the entrance, the scene changes.
Inside, the place feels like a good British pub—a long
bar, with an impressive array of imported beers on tap,
runs the length of the room. Two young women, students from the local university, sit on tall, leather stools
with frosty mugs of beer at their fingertips.

We find a table in the dining room, where a slate floor
and wood-beamed ceiling add to the tavern's ambiance.
In moments, a half-liter of *Tocai* arrives. The fruity bouquet and exciting dry flavor make this regional wine
one of my favorites.

For a light alternative to pasta, Kevin and I study a
refrigerated display case teeming with chilled salads and
fruit. We both decide on *insalata di riso*, thick, chewy
Arborio rice, chopped green peppers, peas, carrots, and
black olives. This Italian rice is different from the kind
we eat in the U.S.: Arborio is plump and doesn't fall
apart in cooking, making even cold dishes taste great.

For my next course, I try *vitello e tonno*, veal with
tuna sauce. Prior to cooking, the veal is marinated 24
hours in white wine, vinegar, and spices. It's served in

thin slices, chilled, with a sauce of olive oil, chopped anchovies, boiled eggs, and tuna. What a taste sensation!

Kevin has *stinco*—an unfortunate name for such a tasty dish. These shins of beef are like spare ribs, and Kevin picks up the meaty bones covered in a delicious tomato sauce and gnaws on them for a long time.

A portion of the Renaissance wall remains across the street from Alla Vigna, and we stroll there after lunch amidst the ancient, crumbling bricks.

Alla Baracca

Via Monti Lessini, 165
Verona
Phone: 521-195
Hours: noon-2:30pm, 7:00pm-10:00pm. Closed
  Saturday.
Cover charge: 1,000 lire/person. No service charge.
Cost of our meal: 31,000 lire
Wheel chair negotiable. &

The beautiful, walled city of Verona is home to the
memory of "Romeo and Juliet," to the second largest
Roman arena (Rome's Colosseum is the largest), and
to Alla Baracca. Perhaps it's odd to add a humble restaurant to a list of such historical import, but Alla Baracca
has provided inexpensive pleasure and sustenance to its
patrons for years, and it's less than two miles from the
city center.

Big and airy, the dining room has plenty of green
plants and picture windows with lace curtains. Fifteen
tables are elegantly set with white linen and long-stem
wine goblets.

We sit in a corner, watching the activity around us.
It's Sunday, and family groups begin to filter in shortly
after the noon hour, dressed in their church finery.
Grandma is always in the lead, wearing a black dress
and tightly combed bun.

Since Veneto is rice country, Kevin and I eagerly try
today's special, *risotto con i finocchi*, rice with fennel.
Unlike rice dishes in America, Italian *risotto* is eaten
as a first course. This recipe is complex—Arborio rice,
sweet fennel slices, and onion gently fried in butter until translucent. The cook adds stock slowly, a cup at a
time, until the rice has absorbed most of the liquid but

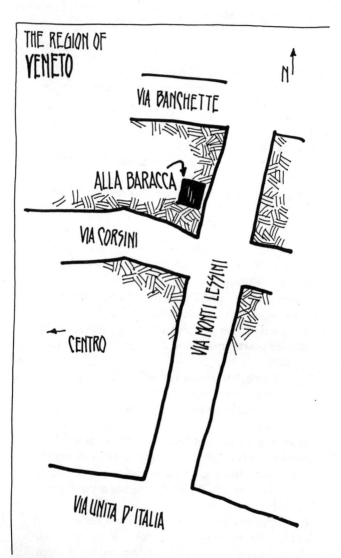

THE REGION OF
VENETO

N↑

VIA BANCHETTE

ALLA BARACCA

VIA CORSINI

VIA MONTI LESSINI

← CENTRO

VIA UNITÀ D' ITALIA

 ALLA BARACCA

VERONA

still has a little "bite." As we indulge in this creamy dish, we agree that the chefs at Alla Baracca took plenty of time and care to create it.

But what would a great Italian dish be without wine? The local grape today is *Soave*, a crisp, white wine produced nearby.

Our next pick is *bocconcini di vitello*, diced veal cooked with tomatoes and a variety of herbs— rosemary, oregano, and marjoram. The result is a sensational stew. Alla Baracca adds slices of *polenta* to every meat dish. With crispy crust on the outside and steamy, corn-based porridge inside, it's a delicious accompaniment.

We bask in the afternoon sunlight, finishing our wine and savoring the flavor of Alla Baracca.

THE REGION OF
VENETO

N↑

CENTRO ↑

PIAZZA

VIALE DELLA VITTORIA

← DAL MORO

← VERONA

AUTO STRADA - A4

 TRATTORIA DAL MORO

SOAVE

Trattoria Dal Moro

Viale Della Vittoria, 1
Soave
Phone: 768-0204
Hours: noon-2:00pm, 7:00pm-10:00pm. Closed
  Thursday.
Cover charge: 2,000 lire/person. No service charge.
Cost of our meal: 41,000 lire
Wheel chair negotiable. ♿

Since *Soave* wine is known worldwide, we naturally
assumed the town where it's produced would be bus-
tling with activity and commerce. What we find instead
is a sleepy little village fringed with miles of rolling vineyards, but devoid of hotels and restaurants. Fearing we'll
go hungry, I insist we stop at a local deli for "emergency" supplies.

"Where do the locals eat?" I ask the butcher in my
Berlitz Italian.

"Over there," he says, pointing across the road as he
hands me a quarter-pound of salami.

We put the package in the car and walk down a long,
gravel driveway to Trattoria Dal Moro. The dining room
has a noble feel, like a palatial hall. The high ceiling
is accented with wrought iron chandeliers, and the tables are dressed in fine linen and guarded by high-back,
wooden chairs.

Although various *Soave* vintages line the shelves
around the room, we choose the simple table version,
a carafe of the familiar pale yellow, dry wine.

The menu changes daily, and tonight our waitress
recommends *fusilli alla sarda*, long pasta spirals with
a smooth, but somewhat salty, sardine sauce—a favorite
Venetian specialty.

Between our pasta and meat courses, local grape-growers saunter into the bar for a nightcap before returning home. They sit silently, drinking glasses of the wine they help make.

For the second course, we both try *baccalà alla vicentina*, a cod dish named for Vicenza, 15 miles north of Soave. I learn that to prepare this dish, sun-dried cod is soaked in water for two days prior to cooking. And now I finally understand what my grandmother was saying when she thought I was dallying in the bathtub too long as a child: "Get out of there. You're soaking like a piece of *baccalà*!" Once it's plump from soaking (the fish, not me), the cod is stuffed with a sautéed mixture of anchovies, parsley, garlic, onions, and *parmigiano* cheese, then baked in a pool of milk for three hours. The recipe is long, but the results are spectacular—moist, pungently flavored seafood.

For leafy vegetables, we have a bowl of *radicchio rosso*, bright red, slightly bitter lettuce, to which we add oil and vinegar dressing.

After a well-balanced meal of Venetian delicacies, we drive north, passing furrowed fields and castle ruins. We're too full to eat the salami, but if we hadn't stopped for it, we never would have found Dal Moro.

The Region of Liguria

This crescent-shaped area, 30 miles wide and 200 miles long, curves around the gulf of Genoa in northwest Italy. Liguria's most prized source of revenue and support is tourism. The region's warm climate and sandy beaches attract sun-seekers to dozens of seaside villages like Portofino and Cinque Terre, gateway to the Mediterranean. The region's agriculture supports only a few crops—mostly herbs, grapes, and olives. Wedged between the Alps and the gulf, the Ligurian soil is unsuitable for much else.

Over the centuries, Italian cooks have learned to adapt and creatively use whatever fruits the area provides. So it comes as no surprise that the soul of Ligurian cuisine is *pesto*—a sauce made from a home-grown herb, sweet basil. Italians still prepare the tangy pasta topping using traditional methods—grinding (chopping the ingredients would be a sin) basil leaves, garlic, pine nuts, and ewe's milk cheese with pestle and mortar until it forms a thick paste. Then they add Ligurian olive oil, said to be the purest in the world.

Basil plants grow everywhere in Liguria and in anything, from old tomato cans perched on apartment windowsills to a small plot of land next to a gas station along the *autostrada* (highway).

You'll be hard pressed to find a Ligurian *trattoria* that doesn't boast about its *pesto*, but you'll be equally hard pressed to find two sauces that taste exactly alike! Although the ingredients are consistent from recipe to recipe, quantities vary to alter the flavor considerably. Some family recipes call for lots of olive oil, while others

THE REGION OF

LIGURIA

use oil sparingly. Whatever the combination, you'll enjoy discovering a favorite.

Ravioli, small pockets of pasta stuffed with cheese or meat, was invented in this area by Genoan sailors. Since it was important for nothing to go to waste aboard a ship, left-overs from dinner the night before were chopped and stuffed into *ravioli*. Modern recipes can be much more elaborate—pumpkin, spiced beef, and sweetbreads are used—but the concept remains the same. In Ligurian *trattorie*, *ravioli* are often topped with a sauce of *pesto*, walnuts, or meat.

Waters surrounding Liguria provide the fish for *ciuppin* (a cold soup similar to French *bouillabaisse*) and *burrida* (fish stew made with a tomato stock and vegetables). The best Ligurian wine comes from the Cinque Terre—five tiny villages (Monterosso, Vernazza, Corniglia, Manarola, and Riomaggiore) clinging to steep cliffs along Italy's eastern Riviera. Monterosso is accessible by car, but the other four fishing towns can be reached only by foot, train, or small boat. Because of a natural rock barricade, the area is cut off from civilization, and the grape-growing land is protected from harsh weather. Although each village produces its own variety of wine (Riomaggiore is said to have the best), most bottles simply read: *"Bianco Secco Delle Cinque Terre"* ("A Dry White Wine of Five Towns"). Another favorite is *Sciacchetrà*, a delicate, fruity white wine.

Whether you come to Liguria to enjoy the food or the sunny Riviera, you'll want to stay long enough to get a good dose of both.

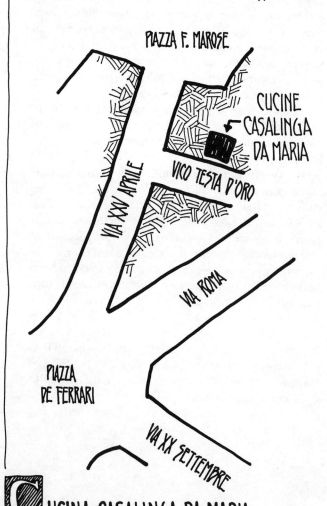

THE REGION OF
LIGURIA

N ↑

PIAZZA F. MAROSE

CUCINE
CASALINGA
DA MARIA

VIA XXV APRILE

VICO TESTA D'ORO

VIA ROMA

PIAZZA
DE FERRARI

VIA XX SETTEMBRE

 CUCINA CASALINGA DA MARIA

GENOA

Cucina Casalinga Da Maria

Vico Testa D'Oro, 14
Genoa
Phone: 571-080
Hours: noon-2:30pm, 7:00pm-9:00pm. Closed Friday
night and all Saturday.
No cover charge. No service charge.
Cost of our meal: 22,500 lire
Not wheel chair negotiable.

Italy's greatest port city, Genoa, on the Ligurian Sea,
is filled with hundreds of eerie, dark passageways so
narrow that it can be difficult for two pedestrians to
make it through side by side. Just north of the Piazza
di Ferrari, down one of these detective-novel alleys, is
a beacon of light—Cucina Casalinga Da Maria. The apt
name means "Maria's Cozy Kitchen," and as soon as we
walk in, we feel we've entered a neighbor's house.

On the first floor, crates of apples and celery muscle-
up to a disorganized front bar. The day's menu, written on strips of paper, hangs banner-style from a wood-
en column. An elderly woman with cherry-red cheeks
smiles at us and points up.

We climb the worn staircase past sacks of potatoes
to the top floor. Paper napkins, bowls of bread, and
a different, flowered cloth dress each of the 12 tables
spread through two rooms.

The food at Cucina Casalinga Da Maria is simple,
regional cuisine—delicious and plentiful. When Kevin
receives his *trenette al pesto*, noodles similar to *fettuccine* smothered in a tangy, green basil sauce, we're sur-
prised to find sliced, boiled potatoes added—a
traditional step that few *trattorie* bother with. It's a wonderful addition and Kevin devours the pasta in
moments.

To ward against the cold, gloomy Genoan night, I order *minestrino in brodo,* thin noodles in a rich chicken broth topped with lots of grated *parmigiano* cheese.

While we enjoy our house wine—*Vaudano,* dry and white—and wait for the next course, an elderly sea captain straight out of *Moby Dick* lumbers up the stairs, wheezing with every step. Twenty years of beer packed inside his uniform leads the way. When he finally reaches the top, he carefully hangs his cap on a corner hook and sits down.

"Hey Bobby!" he gruffly calls the waiter in Italian. "You got any rice with tomato sauce tonight?"

"Well, it's not on the menu, but I can have Mom make you some," Bobby answers. He sticks his head inside the shaft of a dumb waiter and yells to his mother cooking in the kitchen downstairs.

"And tell her to give me a lot of cheese, too," the captain orders. Moments later, we hear the hum of the small elevator and, like magic, a bowl of steaming rice covered in a bright red sauce arrives at his table.

Our second course comes soon after. My *cotolette,* a thin, breaded veal cutlet lightly fried in butter and served with lemon wedges, is crispy and flavorful. Kevin's *arrosto al forno* is a large chunk of pork roasted with vegetables and served in its own juice.

As we exit, laughing about the captain and praising Da Maria's food and service, the lonely alleys seem a little narrower—or are we a little wider?

Trattoria La Buca

Via Chiossone, 5
Genoa
Phone: 294-810
Hours: noon-2:30pm, 7:30pm-11:30pm. Closed
Sunday.
Cover charge: 2,500 lire/person. No service charge.
Cost of our meal: 37,000 lire
Wheel chair negotiable. &

With a worn mosaic floor, dark panelled walls, and
stained-glass windows, walking into Trattoria La Buca
is like entering a Renaissance castle.

Though located in Genoa, the heart of Liguria, La
Buca specializes in Tuscan cuisine—evident by the
pyramid of *Chianti* bottles, Tuscany's most beloved
wine, near the front door. But La Buca offers plenty
of local dishes as well.

With this in mind, Kevin and I each pick a region
and eat according to tradition. I try *minestrone alla
genovese*, a thick vegetable soup with a spoonful of
pesto added before serving. Even though it's a Ligurian dish, beans are the dominant ingredient—a favorite
of Tuscans. I like the blending of the two styles and drink
the soup instantly.

Kevin moves to the region further south, and orders
pasta e fagioli, small, flat noodles with a tomato/bean
sauce. The slight hint of herbs—a Ligurian touch—
makes a tasty combination.

The streets around La Buca are dark and quiet—like
most of Genoa at night—but inside, it's warm and
friendly. Our young waitress giggles as she points to
her tongue when I ask her what *lingua* is. I crinkle my
nose; she does the same, and then suggests we have

THE REGION OF
LIGURIA

N↑

VIA LUCCOLI

VICO CASANA

VIA CHIOSSONE

LA BUCA

VIA S. MATTEO

PIAZZA
DE FERRARI

RATTORIA LA BUCA

GENOA

stufato alla genovese—beef stew. The meat is so tender, it falls apart when Kevin touches his fork to it. We also order their equally good *scaloppine in scobeccio*, breaded veal filets, baked, but served chilled with an onion/lemon sauce. The *insalata mista*, mixed green salad, is wonderful, too—fresh fennel slices, butter lettuce, and tomatoes.

Kevin and I enjoy the rest of our house wine—a light, dry, white *Bico Grabella*—and then return to the sleepy streets of Genoa.

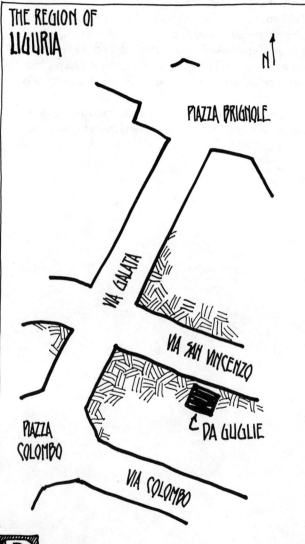

THE REGION OF
LIGURIA

N↑

PIAZZA BRIGNOLE

VIA GALATA

VIA SAN VINCENZO

PIAZZA COLOMBO

DA GUGLIE

VIA COLOMBO

DA GUGLIE

GENOA

Da Guglie

Via San Vincenzo, 64
Genoa
Phone: 565-765
Hours: noon-3:00pm, 7:00pm-10:30pm. Closed
   Sunday.
Cover charge: 1,500 lire/person. No service charge.
Cost of our meal: 30,000 lire
Not wheel chair negotiable.

At noon, the Via Vincenzo in downtown Genoa is bus-
tling with hungry school kids and hurried business executives. The aroma of garlic and oregano from nearby
pizza and *panini* (sandwich) shops tempts a few people, but most head down the street to Da Guglie.

To reach the dining room, we walk down a long hallway. On the way, we pass a room where the tempera-
ture is at least 110 degrees, and a man in a white uniform
and droopy chef's cap is tending pizzas inside a dome-
shaped, brick oven. Next, we peek into the kitchen,
where a woman alternates between chopping vegetables and stirring pots of pasta. She shouts *"Buon giorno!"* to us through a thick cloud of steam.

The back room is crowded: an old man in a beret
sits alone in the corner, sipping a cup of *espresso*, sur-
veying the customers with a watchful eye; office workers devour bowls of spaghetti, never looking up from
their newspapers. We take our seats in the middle of
this group and strain to see the chalk board menu hanging on the opposite wall.

Kevin begins with a favorite Ligurian specialty, *pansoti in salsa di noci*, very thin pockets of pasta—similar
to *ravioli*, only in a crescent moon shape—stuffed with
wild herbs and covered with a walnut sauce. Although

we always share bites, Kevin thinks my fork is approaching his plate too often. I can't help it—the crunchy sauce is exquisite with the delicate *pansoti*. He insists I wait patiently for my first course—*pizza con prosciutto*. When it arrives, I tear off a piece for Kevin and proceed to eat the rest of the pie with tomato sauce, *mozzarella* cheese, and thin slices of cured ham.

My attention is easily diverted from my empty plate to the waitress carrying steaming bowls of something smelling wonderful. I immediately order one for my next course. The mysterious spiced food is *bollito in salsa verde* (beef stew). The small chunks of tender meat, carrots, and potatoes are the best I've ever tasted.

Kevin is pleased, too. His *pollo arrosto*, a breast of chicken baked with fresh rosemary, keeps him busy and, thankfully, away from my stew.

The house wine *Vaudano*—a light, dry white wine from the northern hilltowns—flows easily from carafe to glass to mouth. But, at lunch time we limit ourselves to a half-carafe.

After this feast, we return to Via Vincenzo only to find the street deserted. It's *siesta* time. We're tempted to head back to the hotel for a nap, but we hit the pavement instead to search for another culinary hot-spot.

Trattoria Al Pergolato

Via Torino, 114
La Spezia
Phone: 715-251
Hours: noon-2:30pm, 7:00pm-10:00pm. Closed
  Monday.
Cover charge: 2,000 lire/person. No service charge.
Cost of our meal: 38,000 lire
Wheel chair negotiable. &

The busy seaport of La Spezia along Italy's eastern
Riviera is bursting with *trattorie*, but Kevin and I fight
the temptation and head inland, away from tourist
menus and souvenir stands.

At first, we think Trattoria Al Pergolato, with a big
gelati sign hanging outside, is merely an ice-cream shop.
But just past the vineyard-covered gazebo, hiding behind a picnic table, is an extensive menu with lots of
pasta dishes, including *pesto*.

Al Pergolato is low on decor but high on local color.
Six tables squeeze into one room. The once-white stucco walls have been panelled and display paint-by-
number quality artwork. The main decorative nuance
dangles from the ceiling—a large, neon-blue, bug
zapper.

We look past these small indiscretions and concen-
trate on something more important—the Italian bread
placed on our table. Crunchy on the outside, moist but
not doughy on the inside, we can taste a touch of whole-
wheat flour, and we think it's some of the best bread
we've had.

Since we're in the region of Liguria—*pesto* country—
it's only natural to try Al Pergolato's *penne al pesto*,
long, tubular noodles topped with the bright green,

THE REGION OF
LIGURIA

N ↑

TRAIN
STATION

PIAZZALE
CADUTI P. LAVORO

VIA FIUME

VIA TORINO

AL PERGOLATO

CENTRO
↓

TRATTORIA AL PERGOLATO

LA SPEZIA

tangy basil sauce. We time it so we have just enough bread to soak up the *pesto* remaining in the bottom of our bowls.

Between courses, we sip our wine—the light, white wine of Cinque Terre—and admire the chef's baby, sound asleep on a basket of freshly washed table linens.

All the cheek-pinching and toe-wiggling stops when the food arrives at our table. My *bianchetti fritti*, a variety of small fish—sardines, anchovies, white bait, all batter-dipped and deep-fried—is crunchy and tastes great. Kevin is too consumed with his *burrida* (fish stew) to hear my praises, but he lets me sample his seafood-laden soup made with tomatoes, wine, walnuts, and pieces of toasted bread—an ingenious combination.

After lunch, we return to the port and watch the boats bobbing on the Ligurian Sea, waiting to supply the town with fresh seafood.

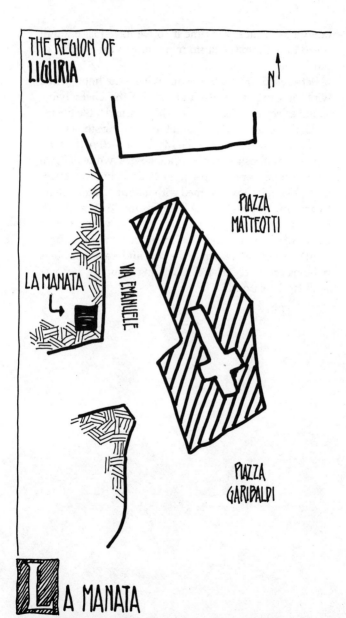

THE REGION OF
LIGURIA

N ↑

PIAZZA
MATTEOTTI

LA MANATA

VIA EMANUELE

PIAZZA
GARIBALDI

LA MANATA

MONTEROSSO AL MARE

La Manata

Via Emanuele, 7
Monterosso al Mare
Phone: 818-167
Hours: noon-2:00pm, 7:00pm-midnight. Closed
   Monday.
Cover charge: 3,000 lire/person. No service charge.
Cost of our meal: 52,000 lire
Outside patio is wheel chair negotiable. &

The Cinque Terre are five tiny villages clinging to vineyard-covered mountains along Italy's eastern Riviera. Monterosso al Mare, the largest of the five, is easy to reach by car, while the other four lay hidden in hillside folds, accessible only by dirt road, train, hiking trail, or fishing boat. Monterosso has two sections: the beach-front strip, lined with small resorts; and the old town with pastel-colored homes climbing rocky foothills, where residents live.

At sunset, Kevin and I stroll through the main square at the waterfront. The kids are playing soccer and the women gossip, out of ear-shot, near the church. It's mid-September, harvest time, and the air is heavy with the smell of fermenting grapes.

Rain begins to fall lightly, so we take refuge at La Manata. The inside dining room is closed, but seeing its red and black plaid wallpaper, I'm somewhat relieved. Instead, we sit outside on a covered platform, pressed against the side of the church. Every hour, the bell sounds, causing our water goblets to shake from the vibration.

We start with a big, frosty liter of Cinque Terre wine. It's a pale white wine with a delicate bouquet and dry flavor, a perfect accompaniment to my *spaghetti con vongole*—pasta, a spicy tomato sauce, and lots of baby clams. Kevin is delighted with his *penne al quattro formaggi*, long, tubular noodles in a creamy sauce of cheeses: *gorgonzola*, *mozzarella*, *fontina*, and *provolone*.

After the owner clears our plates, he walks to the front door of the restaurant, stops halfway out, and looks to the sky. With arms outstretched, his face splashed with rain, he begins to sing. Two waiters from the pizzeria next door, bored from the lack of business, run over to join him. When they finish their song, a dozen customers and passers-by applaud. Once his curtain call is complete, the owner returns to the kitchen for our second course.

Kevin tries *coniglio alla cacciatora*, rabbit stew in a zesty tomato sauce. I opt for more seafood and order *pesce spada al verde*, a thick, grilled swordfish brushed with spicy peppers, onions, and garlic.

After dinner, we wander aimlessly through the twisting, narrow streets of Monterosso. All is quiet except for the hum of homemade wine distilleries concealed behind the unmarked doors.

Il Baretto

Via Roma, 31
Vernazza
Phone: 812-381
Hours: noon-2:30pm, 7:30pm-11:30pm. Closed
   Monday.
Cover charge: 2,500 lire/person. No service charge.
Cost of our meal: 51,000 lire
Outside patio is wheel chair negotiable. ♿

Kevin and I arrive in Vernazza by train, just a two-minute ride from Monterosso, where we're staying. It's 6:00pm, shortly after *siesta* but before dinner. Italians call this time *passeggiata*—the evening stroll—a chance for everyone to meet outside, gossip, and check-up on the neighborhood.

Down at the port, colorful fishing boats docked for the evening bob to the gentle surf. Curiosity-seekers sit along a rock wall and watch the fishermen untangle their nets. Everywhere people are walking arm-in-arm. Kevin and I join in, trying hopelessly to look like natives, but the powerful aroma of pasta from Il Baretto convinces us it's time to eat, even if we're a little early.

Beneath a canvas dome lit softly by spotlight, we people-watch while deciding what to order first. Our waitress brings a carafe of cold Cinque Terre wine. It's slight, characteristic bite awakens my taste buds for the feast ahead.

I start my meal with *gnocchi con pesce*, small dumplings served in a seafood/tomato sauce. Kevin orders *muscoli ripieni*, large, steamed mussels stuffed with bread crumbs and ham, surrounded by a bright red, fresh tomato sauce. The tender seafood and lightly smoked meat complement each other perfectly, but we

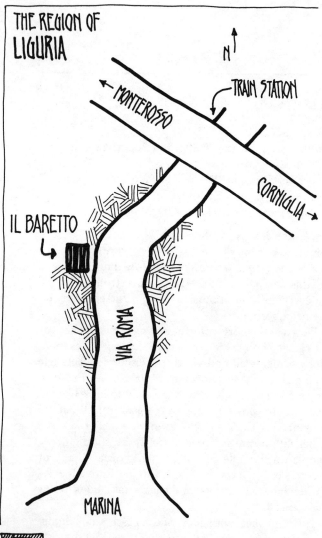

THE REGION OF
LIGURIA

N ↑

MONTEROSSO

TRAIN STATION

CORNIGLIA →

IL BARETTO

VIA ROMA

MARINA

L BARETTO

VERNAZZA

can't figure out how they neatly packed the mixture into the tight shell!

Between courses, we watch the action increase along Via Roma, the village's main passageway. A group of men gather around an accordion player at a nearby cafe. They begin to sing Italian folk songs, softly at first, but as their wine drinking increases, so does their volume. In time, the band moves toward the train station and onto the platform. Then a crowd forms to get a glimpse of the musical troupe. When the Friday night "La Spezia Express" arrives, the happy singers pile inside. The door closes and, for the first time all day, Vernazza is quiet. Kevin says, "That's going to be some ride!"

Turning our attention back to the menu, we each order a type of *pesce a ferri* (grilled fish). I choose red mullet; Kevin opts for swordfish. Both are flaky and juicy, dressed with a sprinkling of herbs. For a side dish, I spot another Ligurian specialty, *crocchette*. Made with rice, cheese, and eggs, these dumplings, the size of eggs, are sautéed in butter and melt in my mouth.

After dinner, we return to the silent port. Candles flicker from cafe tables, and only a few people are about. The fishermen are still untangling their nets, but now they have the help of Vernazza's young women, eager to have them stop working.

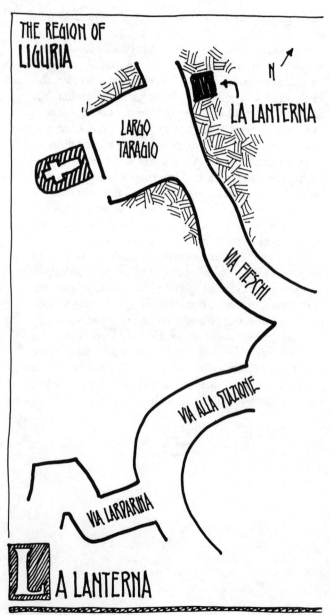

THE REGION OF
LIGURIA

N

LARGO
TARAGIO

LA LANTERNA

VIA FIESCHI

VIA ALLA STAZIONE

VIA LARDARINA

LA LANTERNA

CORNIGLIA

La Lanterna

Via Fieschi, 72
Corniglia
Phone: 812-291
Hours: open daily 12:30pm-3:00pm, 7:00pm-midnight.
Cover charge: 3,000 lire/person. No service charge.
Cost of our meal: 43,000 lire
Not wheel chair negotiable.

The only way to reach Corniglia, the third Cinque Terre village, is to climb a mile-long staircase starting at the train station and zig-zagging up a mountain. We slowly make our way to the top (it takes about 20 minutes), imagining a cool carafe of wine waiting for us. Along the journey, we pass Italians resting under shade trees, snacking on figs and enjoying the view of the ocean hundreds of feet below. Local grape-growers whisk past us, balancing huge baskets of the plump, green fruit on their heads.

Once we reach the summit and catch our breath, we meander the few blocks to the center of town, a rocky plateau fringed with miles of vineyards.

We find La Lanterna down a narrow side street, a peninsula hundreds of feet above sea level running parallel with the coastline. Sheltered in a *piazza*, it shares its space with a weathered old church. We sit outside under sycamore trees and large white umbrellas. Examining the building's stone facade, I think La Lanterna is small, but on my way to the ladies' room I discover otherwise. Downstairs, built against the side of a cliff, is the main dining area—a large room with wood-beam ceiling, surrounded on three sides by a commanding vista of grape fields sloping down to the pounding surf.

La Lanterna specializes in fresh fish. Kevin orders *spaghetti mare*, pasta in a light tomato sauce, topped with mussels, clams, and shrimp. I choose *penne al sugo di scampi*, long, cylindrical noodles, unpeeled shrimp and plenty of tomato sauce for bread-dunking. The bright red sauce covers my face and hands as I peel the seafood, but the meat is so succulent I don't mind a bit.

Between courses we sip local Cinque Terre wine— this delightfully light, dry white wine is everywhere along the Riviera—and watch the locals, deeply tanned from the seaside sun, walk by the *trattoria*, shouting "*Ciao!*" to the waiter who's too busy to notice. He's chasing hungry stray cats away from his customers. These felines know the seafood is fresh, too.

For seconds, *pesce alla griglia*, grilled fish of the day, is presented on a bed of lettuce and dressed with a sprinkling of herbs. Our waiter bones the flounder at our table. The cats trot after him as he carries the bone back inside the restaurant.

At the end of our feast, Kevin and I continue down the alley until we reach a look-out point above the water. Delectable seafood and Corniglia's rugged coast—what more could you ask for?

Trattoria La Grotta

Via Colombo, 123
Riomaggiore
Phone: 920-187
Hours: noon-2:30pm, 7:00pm-11:00pm. Closed
  Wednesday.
Cover charge: 2,000 lire/person. No service charge.
Cost of our meal: 49,000 lire
Wheel chair negotiable. &

We arrive in Riomaggiore, the smallest of the Cinque
Terre villages, the day before *Festa dell'Uve*, the Feast
of the Grapes. Of the five towns, Riomaggiore makes
the best vintages and so hosts the two-day carnival.

The town is humming with activity, as locals busily
decorate the streets with colorful streamers. Wherever
space provides—against stone and mortar walls, in front
of the vegetable stands—crudely painted murals depict
the wine-making process.

From the front patio of Trattoria La Grotta, we watch
the old women of the town argue about who's in charge.
One lady, dressed in a blue housecoat and kerchief,
hangs a three-dimensional, cardboard grape cluster
from a street lantern. As soon as her back is turned,
another lady pulls it down.

Before touching a menu, we order a half-carafe of
Riomaggiore's white table wine and savor its crisp, dry
flavor. We finish our first course—two bowls of *penne
e salmone*, smoked salmon blended into cream sauce,
covering long, tubular noodles—by wiping the rich
sauce from our plates with bread freshly sliced from big,
crusty loaves.

La Grotta is packed with people on this sunny, autumn afternoon. Though a musical soundtrack plays

THE REGION OF
LIGURIA

N ↑

↑ TRAIN STATION

TUNNEL STAZIONE FS CENTRO PAESE

VIA COLOMBO

LA GROTTA

MARINA

TRATTORIA LA GROTTA

RIOMAGGIORE

loudly, we can't hear it over the noise from a huge ceiling fan rotating at top speed to cool the cave-like room, with low, curved, stucco walls. The front counter is decorated with wheels of cheese, baskets of fresh figs, and, naturally, a bowl of plump green grapes.

Kevin orders *calamari frutti*, a delectable dish of bite-size pieces of squid dipped in egg batter and deep-fried. I have *sogliola*, fresh sole grilled quickly then brushed with pine nut and butter sauce just before serving. It's wonderfully moist and flavorful, but La Grotta doesn't score high on presentation—the whole fish, simply sliced open, is brought to the table. l carefully bone it—a little messy, but worth every delicate mouthful. With our fish dishes, we share a plate of sliced, ripe tomatoes. Kevin dresses them with a pinch of salt, a little pepper, and a drizzling of olive oil—perfect!

After lunch, we continue to stroll Via Colombo, examining the decorations for tomorrow's party. Unfortunately, we won't be there—on to another city, another *trattoria*.

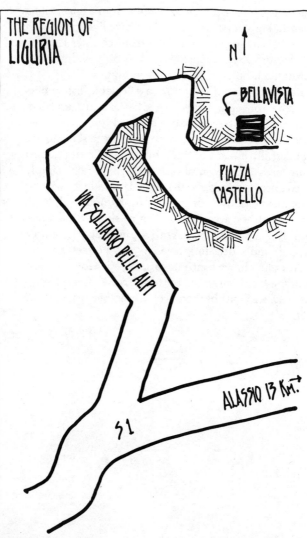

THE REGION OF
LIGURIA

N

BELLAVISTA

PIAZZA
CASTELLO

VIA SOLITARIO PELLE ALPI

ALASSIO 13 KM.

S1

BELLAVISTA

CERVO

Bellavista

Piazza Castello, 2
Cervo
Phone: 408-094
Hours: open daily noon-2:30pm, 7:00pm-11:00pm.
  Closes in late fall; reopens at Christmas.
Cover charge: 2,000 lire/person. No service charge.
Cost of our meal: 32,000 lire
Not wheel chair negotiable.

After the hustle and noise of Italy's large cities, Kevin and I search for solitude along Italy's western Riviera. Although free from fast-paced urban dwellers, it's crowded with sun-seekers. Turning our eyes upward, we scan the hillsides, dreaming of a small oasis.

Just past Alassio on Via Giugno, clinging to a rocky mountain, a church steeple rises through a cluster of houses. "This is it!" I shout. "Turn here!" We drive through tiers of olive trees until we reach Cervo—a remote village built around San Giovanni Battista, a 12th-century church.

Outside the city is Bellavista, a hotel complete with *trattoria*. From large picture windows in Bellavista's dining room, we watch the sun dip behind distant western peaks, as the sea below turns from blue to purple to black.

The *signora* cooks our pasta to order while she and her family watch a soccer game on television. As we eat our first course—*penne con bottarge*, cylinder-shape pasta covered with a sauce of salty anchovies, chopped tomatoes, and olive oil; and *penne ai carciofi*, the same type of noodles tossed in a mild artichoke purée—we hear shouts of joy from the kitchen. The soccer game was obviously as good as our food.

After a brief post-game discussion, we're served the second course. I dive into my *fritture mista del golfo*, a variety of fresh seafood lightly battered and deep-fried. The plate is piled so high, I need assistance from Kevin after he's devoured his *scaloppine al marsala*, thin, breaded veal fillets simmered in sweet Italian wine.

When we're finished we retire to the outside patio for an after-dinner martini. We drink from our pleasant hilltop perch, lulled by the lights of the Riviera below. The stress of city traveling fades into the darkness, and the quiet night and gourmet meal make us sleepy. We vow to return someday.

Trattoria Da Antonio

Via Aurelia, 87
San Bartolomeo al Mare
Phone: 400-314
Hours: noon-2:00pm, 7:00pm-11:00pm. Closed
  Wednesday.
Cover charge: 2,500 lire/person. No service charge.
Cost of our meal: 46,000 lire
Wheel chair negotiable. &

With one tourist resort after another lining Italy's western Riviera, it's hard to find good, traditional cooking, but a local beach comber suggested his favorite spot, Trattoria Da Antonio.

Like most family-run establishments, it's small and simple. Picnic tables and Coca-Cola signs decorate the outside; the inside is just a narrow room with eight tables and a kitchen.

For starters, Kevin and I share *zuppa di pesce*, a huge bowl of fish soup overflowing with steamed mussels, clams, shrimp, and scallops in a spicy, tomato broth. After it's served, our waitress slices a basket of bread from a large collection hidden behind the bar. We use all the crunchy, thin-crusted *pane* to soak up the salty juice left in the tureen.

Still in a seafood mood, I ask our waitress what type of fish is available. She recites a list, but unfortunately my Italian vocabulary isn't as big as my appetite. "I'm sorry, I don't understand," I say in Italian.

"*Un momento, signora,*" she responds, and disappears into the kitchen. Moments later she returns carrying a small, silver platter with a beautiful, eight-inch, gray fish.

"*Va bene,*" I say, smiling. With my approval, she exits with my soon-to-be-dinner.

THE REGION OF
LIGURIA

N ↑

VIA ROMA

ALASSIO →

S1

IMPERIA ←

DA ANTONIO ←

VIA SARDEGNA

 RATTORIA DA ANTONIO

SAN BARTOLOMEO AL MARE

We wait patiently and sip our Cinque Terre wine. The majority of patrons tonight are families. Mom and Dad sit at the ends of the tables, with large pots of seafood anchored in the center. No one talks—they're too busy cracking crab claws between their teeth and slurping the juicy meat from the shells.

The waitress rolls a cart to our table, displaying my grilled fish. After boning it, she places the delicate fillet on a plate and spoons olive oil and lemon sauce over it. Although Kevin is slightly envious of the fuss for my one fish, he's delighted with his *scaloppine al limone*, a breaded strip of veal sautéed in butter and served with lemon wedges.

Stuffed and satisfied, we leave Da Antonio just as the chef emerges to rest and eat his dinner. He shouts *"Arrivedérci!"* from the corner table as his wife pours him a glass of red wine. I want to tell him I loved the fish, but I'm still not sure what kind it was!

THE REGION OF

OMBARDY

The Region of Lombardy

Lombardy, in north-central Italy, is a region of sharp contrasts. To the north, just over the border from Switzerland, the Alps soar to heights over 13,000 feet. Cradled below is the Italian Lake District—six finger-like pools punctuated with tiny, alpine villages.

Traveling south, though, toward the culinary capital Milan, the landscape quickly changes into miles of endless rice fields and cow pastures. While the north is a vacationer's paradise, the south is strictly business.

Lombardy is Italy's largest agricultural producer, explaining their love for butter—the principle cooking fat—and *gorgonzola*, a creamy, bitter cheese produced in a small town of the same name, ten miles east of Milan.

Milanese are passionate about rice, first introduced there in the 1400's. Soon after, saffron—an herb that looks, and costs, like gold—found its way into Milan's kitchens. The combination created one of the region's most beloved specialties—*risotto alla milanese*. It's been called "The national dish of Lombardy," and "The gold of Milan." You'll call it delicious.

Though you'll find pasta on *trattorie* menus, there's a more popular first course in Lombardy: *polenta*. Upon first glance, many think this simple mixture of corn meal and water should be eaten at breakfast, like oatmeal, but northern Italians choose to savor its subtle flavor at dinner. Popular ways to prepare it are with local *valtellina* cheese (*polenta taragna*) or baked with a fresh tomato sauce (*polenta pasticciata*).

A friend who lived in Milan once told me that he tried

polenta for the first time at a country picnic. His host offered it to him barbecued—a thick slice of the hardened corn meal grilled and then drizzled with olive oil. After one taste, he was hooked!

Regional specialties reach far beyond the first course, and *osso buco alla milanese* rates high. For this dish, shins of veal—the center bone and its delicious marrow intact—are cooked with wine and tomatoes. Often it's served with *gremolada* sauce—a mixture of lemon juice, anchovies, garlic, rosemary, parsley, and sage.

Lombardy's flatlands provide an abundance of butter, cheese, and rice, but not grapes. They just don't grow well there, but a few local wines worth trying are *Cortese* and *Frecciarossa*—both red and produced near the Po River Valley.

Trattoria Picchio

Corso Como, 2
Milan
Phone: 659-0444
Hours: 11:30am-2:00pm, 7:00pm-10:30pm. Closed
   Tuesday.
Cover charge: 2,000 lire/person. No service charge.
Cost of our meal: 40,000 lire
Not wheel chair negotiable.

Twelve men drinking short glasses of red wine and talking soccer scores fill the dark interior of Trattoria Picchio. Although a menu is posted outside, we can't see a dining room—just a bar, a long deli counter, and a few weathered chairs. As we enter to investigate, the gentlemen step aside to form human walls to a rear staircase.

On the lower floor are seven linen-covered tables. Long white curtains give the impression of windows where there are none (we're in a basement). Between these "windows" are shelves stocked three-deep with wine. At a corner table, a Benedictine monk, drinking an after-dinner *espresso* and smoking a Marlboro, talks quietly with his companion.

We're here for *zuppa alla pavese*—the soup of Pavia, a traditional Lombardy dish that few *trattorie* offer. According to legend, it was created in the 16th century when a nobleman hunting in the hills around Pavia, 30 miles south of Milan, stopped at a farmhouse for lunch. The only food the poor peasant had to offer was chicken soup. Embarrassed, she improvised by adding a chunk of bread, a raw egg, chopped parsley, and grated cheese. The nobleman was so delighted with the new dish he called it "The Soup of Pavia."

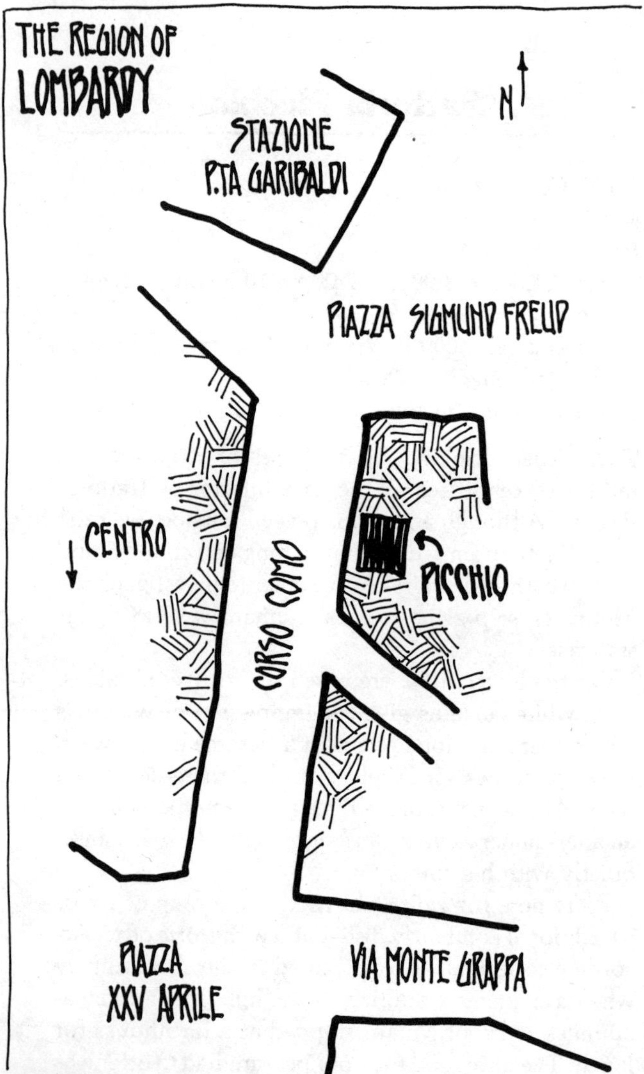

TRATTORIA PICCHIO

MILAN

Two piping-hot bowls arrive with a liter of *Bonarda*, ruby red wine from Piedmont. We slurp down the soup until it's nearly gone, then break the yolk and take more bread to sop it up, with the remaining broth. It's deliciously simple and fun to eat.

With our curiosity satisfied, we move on to the next course. I have *costolette alla milanese*, a thin, breaded veal cutlet pan-fried in butter. Kevin chooses *scaloppine a piacere*, a veal fillet cooked "to his liking." Tonight he has it grilled with lemon wedges. Fresh Lombardy string beans, *cornetti*, quickly sauteed in olive oil and garlic, round-off the meal.

Like the 16th-century nobleman, Kevin and I are happy we stumbled upon Trattoria Picchio and an intriguing soup with an impressive name.

THE REGION OF
LOMBARDY

N↑

CORSO INDIPENDENZA

PIAZZALE
DATEO

 DA BRUNO

VIA MELLONI

← CENTRO

VIA F. BRONZETTI

DA BRUNO

MILAN

Da Bruno

Corso Indipendenza, 20
Milan
Phone: 730-029
Hours: 12:30pm-2:30pm, 7:00pm-11:30pm. Closed
   Sunday.
Cover charge: 1,500 lire/person. No service charge.
Cost of our meal: 36,000 lire
Wheel chair negotiable. ♿

Finding Da Bruno is a bit tricky. Although their printed address claims the eatery is located on Corso Indipendenza, it's actually around the corner on Bronzetti.
Regardless, this low-priced *trattoria* is worth the search.

   Da Bruno is tiny, from ten doll-size tables squeezed
into one room to the front bar, barely wide enough to
accommodate the bartender. It's so small, the bathroom
is outside in a flower-filled courtyard.

   Ironically, the owner of Da Bruno is large, and so are
the food portions. The *padrone*, both arms piled with
plates of food and suspenders strung tightly across his
bulging belly, can hardly maneuver down the center
aisle. But he delivers my *minestrone di riso* without
spilling a drop. The vegetable soup with rice gets its
golden hue from saffron, a favorite regional herb added to many specialties. Kevin keeps it simple and eats
riso e burro, rice with butter, but with special rice called
Arborio. Different than grains at home, this rice can
withstand lots of cooking and still retain a flavorful
"bite."

   Throughout the evening, the *signora* peers from the
kitchen to make sure everyone is enjoying her food. She
doesn't have to worry about us. My next course, *punte
di vitello*, thick slices of roasted veal served in its own

juice, is exceptional.

Before Kevin embarks on his next dish, he orders another half-carafe of *Lugana*, a delicate white wine produced near the southern tip of Lake Garda. With a glass of the local grape at his side, he samples his *arrosto tacchino al forno* (roasted turkey breast), and it's perfect.

The vegetable choices at Da Bruno are extensive. We order *spinaci* (spinach) cooked to our specifications— sauteed with olive oil and garlic.

As we leave the *trattoria*, I remind Kevin to mark the location on his street map. A place this good is one I want everyone to find easily.

Trattoria Blitz

Viale Premuda, 38
Milan
No phone.
Hours: noon-3:00pm, 7:00pm-11:00pm. Closed
   Sunday.
Cover charge: 1,500 lire/person. No service charge.
Cost of our meal: 29,500 lire
Wheel chair negotiable. &

A waitress places two Dolomiti-brand water bottles on
our table. "*Vino*," she says, pointing to the smaller flask.
Wait a minute—wine in a water bottle? Kevin tastes its
contents. "It's wine," he concludes, smacking his lips.
The noon crowd is growing, and the folks at Trattoria
Blitz must improvise when necessary.

We sit back with our incognito bottle of *Volpi*—a
white wine from Cortese—and watch the show. Trattoria Blitz is casual, and lunchtime brings in all the area
workers. Laughter echoes through the long, narrow
room as people move from table to table, like guests
at a party—eating pasta with one group of friends, then
meat with another.

The waitress returns with our first course, chosen
from an illegible chalk board hanging on the wall across
the room. She's a teenager—small and full of energy.
"*Grazie*," I say as she places my *spaghetti arrabbiata* before me.

"*Niente!* (It's nothing!)" she replies and bounces back
to the kitchen for another pick-up. The steaming bowl
of pasta, topped with a tomato and red pepper sauce,
is biting but not overpowering. I apologize to Kevin,
who's still waiting for his first course (as often happens
in these small *trattorie* with limited kitchen space), and

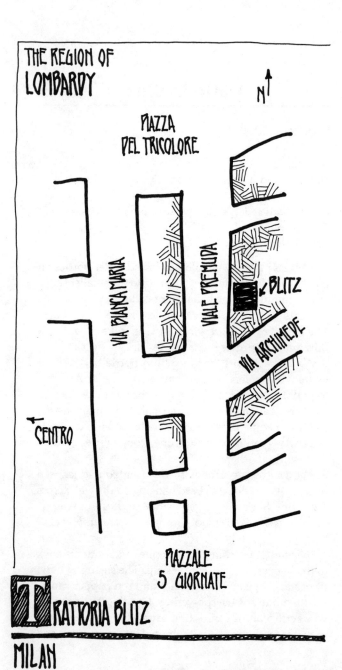

dig into my pasta. But Kevin is soon enjoying *maccheroni con funghi*, long, thin hollow noodles tossed in olive oil and sliced *porcini* mushrooms.

For the next round, Kevin tries something light and snacks on *caprese*, slices of red tomatoes and buffalo milk *mozzarella* cheese. He sprinkles salt, pepper, and a little olive oil on them. The cheese is soft and creamy, the tomatoes ripe and fresh. When all is eaten, he takes bread to wipe up the juice left behind—nothing goes to waste with my husband! I watch his ritual until my *scaloppine marsala* arrives. Then my attention is on the thin veal fillets simmered in sweet, Italian wine.

By 2:00pm, all the local workers are finishing their wine and thinking about where to spend their afternoon *pennicchella* (nap). It's a delightful but puzzling tradition. How does a modern economy function when everyone in the country is "taking a little rest" every afternoon? While pondering the question, we decide to go to our hotel for a nap.

THE REGION OF
LOMBARDY

N

VIA GARIBALDI

VIA C PELLOSIO

GIACOMO ↘

SALITA SERBELLORI

TRATTORIA GIACOMO

BELLAGIO

Trattoria Giacomo

Via Salita Serbelloni, 45
Bellagio
Phone: 950-329
Hours: noon-3:00pm, 7:00pm-11:30pm. Closed
   Sunday.
Cover charge: 2,000 lire/person. No service charge.
Cost of our meal: 50,000 lire
Not wheel chair negotiable.

Bellagio, one of the prettiest destinations in northern
Italy, is surrounded on three slides by Lake Como and
sweeping snow-capped vistas of the Swiss Alps.
Although the restaurants of this lakeside resort cater
to tourists and serve uninspiring pasta dishes, there is
a small, unpretentious *trattoria* offering popular regional specialties.

The focal point inside Trattoria Giacomo is a step-
up bar illuminated by fluorescent lights. Pictures and
panoramic scenes of the magnificent natural setting
decorate the room. Next to the door is a large poster
advertising the latest film playing across the street.

The chef exits the kitchen carrying a small pot. He
greets us with a smile and a nod toward a table. His
tall frame, protruding beer belly, and whimsical atti-
tude remind us of Ed Norton from "The Honeymoon-
ers" television series. "Ed" walks to where his teenage
son is eating dinner and slaps another spoonful of *risotto* on his plate, then returns to the kitchen.

Ruling the front dining area is the *signora*. She's the
only waitress for all nine tables, and she handles the
job competently, bringing us a carafe of wine to enjoy
with our first course. *Barbera*, a deep red, full-bodied,
dry wine, goes well with the evening meal.

Tonight, Trattoria Giacomo has a special *polenta*. This staple of maize and water, cooked slowly until it thickens, can include a variety of ingredients like onions or mushrooms, but we have it plain with melted *fontina* cheese on top. Its mild corn flavor and smooth texture is a cross between porridge and corn bread, only better than either.

Round two is another Lombardy specialty, *osso buco alla milanese*, veal shanks simmered in white wine, tomatoes, and herbs until the meat is tender to the fork's touch. No knives are needed for this delicacy. When we're finished, Kevin scoops out the marrow from the center bone and spreads it on a piece of bread.

"It's the best part," he says smiling. I follow his lead and wholeheartedly agree.

By 9:00pm, the room is filled with tourists. It can't be helped. Trattoria Giacomo has the best deal in town, and word gets around fast.

Trattoria Il Tiglio

Piazza Canestri, 1
Visgnola (Bellagio)
Phone: 951-404
Hours: noon-2:00pm, 7:30pm-10:30pm. Closed
  Monday.
Cover charge: 2,000 lire/person. No service charge.
Cost of our meal: 46,000 lire
Not wheel chair negotiable.

Though the suburb Visgnola is just minutes from the
busy tourist town of Bellagio, Trattoria Il Tiglio is filled
nightly with locals, not tourists.

Kevin and I arrive at 7:00pm, a half-hour before the
cucina (kitchen) is open for business, so we have a glass
of wine and wait and watch. Several children are discussing the pros and cons of vanilla ice cream while
standing in front of a humming freezer against the front
wall. They finally decide on chocolate.

Shopkeepers enter for a quick *espresso* before going
home for the evening. Even an occasional dog wanders
in, sniffing for a scrap or his misplaced owner. All these
scenes add to the lively drama of tiny Il Tiglio's homey
establishment.

At 7:30, we move a few feet from the bar to the dining
area. Like the rest of the *trattoria*, it's simple in style—
six 1950's-style tables with turquoise chairs, its walls
covered with posters of Lapland. Every family mem-
ber has a job. Dad mans the bar, his teenage daughter
(eager to practice her English) is our waitress, while
mom is the chef tonight. She pours herself a glass of
red wine and takes it into the kitchen with her.

We order more wine, too—*Valcalepio*, bright red with
a subtle, dry flavor. It arrives just in time for our first

THE REGION OF
LOMBARDY

N ↑

← BELLAGIO

← VISGNOLA

PIAZZA
CANESTRI

↰ IL TIGLIO

TRATTORIA IL TIGLIO

VISGNOLA

course, two orders of *polenta con brasato*—moist slices of *polenta*, the consistency of corn bread, served with tender braised beef in a rich brown gravy. By the time we finish, we're stuffed. Kevin is content, but I push for another entrée. It's for the good of the book, I tell him. I don't have to twist his arm.

We decide to split an order of *scaloppine con funghi*, thin veal fillets briefly sauteed in olive oil, white wine, and lots of sliced *porcini* mushrooms.

While we eat, the *signora* exits the kitchen to relax for a short time. Like a true Italian, she wants us to en-joy her food, *"Va bene?"* she asks us. I nod approving-ly, my mouth too full to speak. She laughs.

THE REGION OF
LOMBARDY

N↑

CENTRO

VIA DELLA BOCCOLA

← BERNABO

VIA B. COLLEONI

VIA S. SALVATORE

VIA SALVECCHIO

RATTORIA BERNABO

BERGAMO

Trattoria Bernabo

Via B. Colleoni, 31
Bergamo (Alta)
Phone: 237-692
Hours: noon-2:30pm, 7:00pm-midnight. Closed
  Thursday.
Cover charge: 2,000 lire/person. No service charge.
Cost of our meal: 47,000 lire
Wheel chair negotiable. &

Bergamo is located in the middle of Lombardy's *polenta* country, where the versatile maize is the dietary mainstay. Even local pastry shops display their versions — *polenta e osei*, a smooth mound of yellow grain topped with caramel and chocolate sticks.

The city is divided into two distinct parts—*bassa*, the lower, newer area where most people live and work, and *alta*, a walled, hilltop, Renaissance jewel, home of Trattoria Bernabo.

Set in the midst of medieval towers and winding alleys, Bernabo is an inviting, sophisticated inn with tall, domed ceilings and soft, romantic lighting. We sit near the bar, a marble/polished wood showpiece, and watch the bartender carefully eyeball glasses of *grappa* (a distilled spirit made from grape mash).

Breaking our pasta-first habit, we begin with *carpaccio*, a cold dish of raw meat sliced paper thin and served with a drizzle of olive oil and lemon juice. Though named after the famous Venetian painter, the dish originated in Piedmont.

Next, two bowls of *quadruci in brodo di carne*, bite-size, beef-filled *ravioli*, are delicious in clear beef broth. Once every drop is gone, the bowls are immediately whisked away by our waiter—part of a very conscientious staff. Only moments after our half-carafe runs dry, he's back to offer a second. The *Cellatica*, a red, dry, delightful wine, floated so smoothly over our palates, we instantly accept his offer.

Naturally we must try *polenta* as a main course. I have *salsiccia con polenta*, thin pork sausages on a bed of golden maize, while Kevin tries *coniglio alla berganesca con polenta*, small roasted rabbit fillets simmered in white wine sauce, accompanied by a scoop of the creamy porridge.

We close our feast with two cups of *espresso* and agree that dining at Bernabo is worth the long walk to the walled city.

Trattoria Morla

Via Baioni, 2
Bergamo (Bassa)
Phone: 239-087
Hours: noon-3:00pm, 7:00pm-midnight. Closed
  Sunday.
Cover charge: 1,700 lire/person. No service charge.
Cost of our meal: 36,000 lire
Wheel chair negotiable. &

Located in Bergamo's *città bassa* (lower city) near the
university, Trattoria Morla is popular with college students. The large circular dining room is sparsely decorated and uncluttered. Bare light bulbs hang from cords,
bouncing harsh light off the white walls. Customers
don't mind—they're too busy watching the big-screen
television in the corner. Normally, Kevin and I would
try another place to eat, but we know from months of
trattoria-hunting that looks are deceiving. Morla con-
firms the cliché.

A basket of thick, chewy bread and a half-carafe of
Cellatica, a dry red wine from the hills west of neighboring Brescia, are brought to our table, moments after we sit. We devour both before the first course arrives.
Our waitress refills them after she delivers Kevin's *piz-
zoccheri*, a popular but odd-looking dish of long buck-
wheat noodles and vegetables in a creamy cheese sauce.
We ask for the recipe, but somewhere between cabbage
and potatoes, the translation gets muddled. Kevin suggests possible ingredients with each mouthful, while I
enjoy my *risotto con funghi*, Arborio rice and an abundance of *porcini* mushrooms slowly cooked in a rich
beef broth.

Eager for more, my *merluzzo con polenta* (baked,

THE REGION OF LOMBARDY

N ↑

VIA PAGLIONI

VIA LAZZERETTO

MORLA

VIA NAZ. SAURO

CENTRO

TRATTORIA MORLA

BERGAMO

breaded cod with slices of *polenta*) is delicious. Kevin is quick to order *scaloppine al gorgonzola*, sauteed veal fillets with his favorite cheese sauce. The mildly pungent *gorgonzola*, produced in the town of the same name ten miles east of Milan, is fresh and tasty.

Although Trattoria Morla looks a little disorganized, the great food makes it well worthwhile.

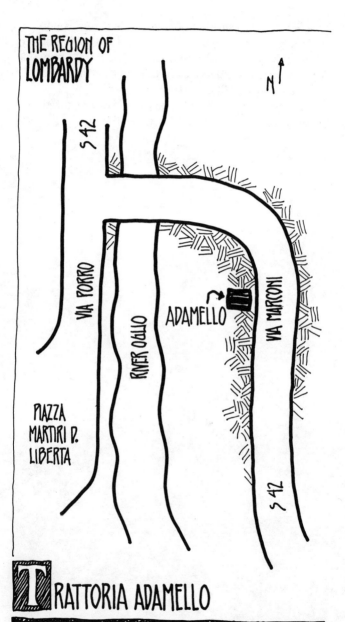

THE REGION OF
LOMBARDY

N

S 42

VIA PORRO

RIVER OGLIO

ADAMELLO

VIA MARCONI

S 42

PIAZZA
MARTIRI D.
LIBERTA

RATTORIA ADAMELLO

EDOLO

Trattoria Adamello

Via Marconi, 18
Edolo
Phone: 71-131
Hours: noon-2:30pm, 7:00pm-11:00pm. Closed
 Sunday.
Cover charge: 2,000 lire/person. No service charge.
Cost of our meal: 39,000 lire
Not wheel chair negotiable.

Edolo, at the eastern tip of the Lombardy region, is a
great base from which to explore the rugged peaks of
the Dolomites. A crystal-clear stream flows through the
center of this sleepy town, feeding Lake Iseo to the
south. The main *piazza* is filled with lunchtime nature-
lovers sunning themselves on park benches. Church
bells announce the noon hour, and our arrival.

We find Trattoria Adamello partially hidden below
street level and only one block from the center square.
Though we're miles from the Austrian border, there's
an Alpine feel in its three dining rooms. Dark slate
floors, wood-beam ceiling, and polished brass lanterns
create an intimate, rustic setting.

The food is hearty, peasant fare. With no set menu,
the dishes change daily according to season and product
availability. We listen carefully to our waiter's list of first
course offerings, and then choose *casoncelli*, plump pasta pockets the size of golf balls, stuffed with ground
meat, potatoes, and *pancetta* bacon. Surprisingly,
they're very light and, with a little olive oil, quite tasty
with our *Terlano*, the yellow, dry wine made in the next
region.

Trattoria Adamello is a family affair. At 1:00pm, two
small children enter through the kitchen door and plop

down at a table. Their father—our waiter—serves them two bowls of soup and a plate of French fries. Meanwhile, the *signora* prepares our next course, *costoletta alla milanese*, veal Milan-style. She pounds the cutlet until it's thin and tender, then dips it into an egg batter and quickly cooks it in butter. It arrives moments later, hot and crispy.

The best is yet to come. For dessert, we treat ourselves to *laciaditt*, batter-dipped apple slices, deep-fried and sprinkled with sugar. Normally, we don't indulge in such naughty delicacies, but we were very good today—we ate all our lunch.

The Region of
Emilia-Romagna

With world-renowned culinary centers like Parma,
Bologna, and the seaside resort of Rimini, the region
of Emilia-Romagna, stretching east-west across Italy's
upper boot, is a food lover's paradise. The people of
this diverse area have a zest for living and a passion
for fine cuisine.

The region's food is rich and robust. Some Italians
say it's heavy, but Emilians claim that description only
indicates jealousy. The use of cheese, cream, pasta,
pork, and calorie-laden lard has earned Emilia-Romagna the nickname *"la grassa,"* the fat one. However,
we didn't notice many overweight Emilians. They seem
to enjoy their riches in moderation.

Two distinct styles of cooking exist here: seafood
dishes of the coastal towns and meat specialties of the
inland areas. Every morning in Rimini, the area's largest fishing village, small, brightly colored boats descend
upon the Adriatic in search of a harvest to dress *trattoria* tables that night. *Brodetto di rimini*, the local fish
soup, combines the daily fresh catch—sole, flounder,
mullet, bass, sardines, squid, and clams—for the best
chowder along the eastern shore.

Inland, the dinner table is set differently. Rich, fer-
tile plains make excellent pork-raising territory.
Prosciutto, slowly cured pig's leg, is the most popular
and prized. *Prosciutto e melone*, paper-thin slices of raw
ham wrapped around wedges of cantaloupe, is a
favorite summertime appetizer. This melt-in-your-

THE REGION OF

MILIA-ROMAGNA

mouth meat is also prominently featured in *tagliatelle al prosciutto*—wide noodles served with a cream/butter sauce and julienne strips of ham. From the city of the same name, Parma ham, mildly smoked, adorns *lombatine alla parmigiana*—sautéed veal fillets dressed with a slice of Parma ham and melted cheese.

If these dishes are unfamiliar, you're sure to recognize the region's top export, *parmigiano reggiano*—a hard, pungent cheese invented over a thousand years ago. Its biting flavor adds distinction to many local specialties, especially pasta.

Prized semolina flour, *sfoglia*, is used exclusively in *tortellini*—bite-sized pockets of stuffed pasta. Some Emilians claim *tortellini* was created by a chef who wanted to immortalize the navel of Venus, the goddess of love. Try this dimpled pasta in *tortellini d'erbetta del parmigiano*, served with butter and cheese, or *tortellini pasticciati alla bolognese*, baked in meat sauce.

You'll find an excellent selection of wine to go with all this good food. *Lambrusco*, though unpopular abroad because it doesn't travel well, smells of violets and is a great complement to spicy food. With fish, try the aromatic, deep red *Sangiovese* from Forli.

If you've come to Italy to eat, be prepared—once you set foot in an Emilian *trattoria*, you may never want to leave!

THE REGION OF
EMILIA-ROMAGNA

N ↑

CENTRO ↗

VIALE YICINI

PIAZZA DI
PORTA SARAGOZZA

VIA SARAGOZZA

VIALE ALDINI

↖ BONI

TRATTORIA BONI

BOLOGNA

Trattoria Boni

Via Saragozza, 88
Bologna
Phone: 585-060
Hours: noon-2:30pm, 7:30pm-midnight. Closed
  Saturday.
Cover charge: 2,000 lire/person. No service charge.
Cost of our meal: 45,500 lire
Wheel chair negotiable. ♿

In the culinary capital Bologna, the folks take their food
seriously, and no where is it more apparent than at Trattoria Boni, located in the southwest corner of the city
along one of the many porticoed streets. The long, narrow restaurant fills to capacity by 9:00pm, so arrive early if you want a seat. Its show is vibrant, starring waiters
dressed in neatly pressed, black-tie uniforms. There's
high spirited chaos among the staff and patrons, complete with fine linen and warm, panelled walls.

The menu offers "new wave" interpretations of the
rich, Emilia-Romagna standards, including *tortellini alla
lista del giorno*. The sauce varies daily depending on
the whim of the chef, but the pasta is always the
same—the region's favorite, *tortellini*, cheese-filled ringlets shaped to immortalize the navel of Venus, goddess
of love.

We try two off-beat items. First, *passatelli alla romag-
nola*, wiggly, string-like pasta made from *parmigiano*
cheese, bread crumbs, and eggs. They serve it in a small
amount of chicken broth to complement the tangy
cheese flavor, not overpower it. Our other first course
is *fettuccine alla rucola*—long, flat noodles with a
smoky *pancetta* cream sauce. A liter of *Prosecco*, a dry
white wine produced in the hills south of Bologna, ac-

companies these piquant dishes.

The room pumps with energy. Waiters whiz along, plates suspended the length of both arms. The clientele is a great mix, from ladies in fur coats to groups of pony-tailed men toasting their future careers as musicians.

We watch the action but also anticipate our next course—*cotoletta alla bolognese*. These thin, breaded veal cutlets are topped with slices of *prosciutto* and *par-migiano* cheese, then baked in tomato sauce and red wine.

For dessert, we order *dolce bologna*—a sinfully rich dessert consisting of chocolate and vanilla mousse layered between liquor-soaked sponge cake and topped with *espresso*.

Dining at Trattoria Boni is great fun, from the hum of the crowd to the taste of Bologna's wonderful, fattening food. It's not to be missed.

Trattoria Da Danio

Via S. Felice, 50
Bologna
Phone: 555-202
Hours: 11:30am-3:00pm, 6:30pm-11:30pm. Closed
  Sunday.
Cover charge: 3,000 lire/person. No service charge.
Cost of our meal: 35,000 lire
Not wheel chair negotiable.

From the homemade pasta at rock-bottom prices to the
cast of eccentric, lunchtime locals, Trattoria Da Danio
is a must in downtown Bologna.

Like many restaurants in town, Da Danio is long, narrow, and simple in decor: two rows of linen-covered tables, dozens of coat racks along the walls, and
multi-colored, plastic wainscoting throughout the
dining room. Moments after we sit down, a short, balding waiter shuffles to our table and slaps a roll on each
plate. He leans down, putting his ear inches from my
mouth to catch my order of a carafe of *Colli Bolognesi*,
deep red with a gentle, dry taste, produced in the outlying Bolognese hills.

Like an American 1950's diner, Da Danio offers a
daily special, and today it's *maccheroni al forno*—baked
macaroni. Sound familiar? However, Da Danio's recipe
calls for ground meat, onions, white wine, tomatoes,
and *mozzarella*—not cheddar cheese. Kevin manages
to steal a bite before his *lasagne verdi al forno* arrives.
The pyramid of spinach noodles, layered with *ricotta*
cheese and tomato sauce, is a meal in itself.

All afternoon, a strange mix of "regulars" files in for
the noon meal. From the aging beauty queen with heavily made-up eyes and drooping cheeks to the gentleman

THE REGION OF
EMILIA-ROMAGNA

N ↑

VIA RIVA DI RENO

CENTRO ↘

VIA SAN FELICE

VIA PIETRALATA

DA DANIO ↱

VIA PARADISO

TRATTORIA DA DANIO
BOLOGNA

with a cowboy hat and cane, all are loudly greeted by name by our deaf waiter as they take their assigned seats.

We quietly giggle at this scene but quickly settle down at the arrival of our *lombo di maiale al forno*, roasted loin of pork. This, coupled with our *piselli* (fresh sweet peas), rivals any "Blue Plate Special."

Simple, tasty food and an unusual eating environment makes Da Danio a culinary adventure worth taking.

THE REGION OF
EMILIA—ROMAGNA

N ↑

PIAZZA
VIII AGOSTO

VIA AUGUSTO RIGHI

VIA DELL' INDIPENDENZA

↰ TONY

↓ CENTRO

 RATTORIA TONY

BOLOGNA

Trattoria Tony

Via A. Righi, 1
Bologna
Phone: 232-852
Hours: noon-2:30pm, 7:00pm-11:30pm. Closed
    Tuesday.
Cover charge: 3,000 lire/person. No service charge.
Cost of our meal: 50,000 lire
Wheel chair negotiable. ♿

Trattoria Tony, located off the beautiful, porticoed Via dell' Independenza, reminds Kevin and me of a New York City restaurant—crowded, noisy, and smoky. The brightly lit dining room is long, narrow, and rather cramped. A center aisle acts as a two-way freeway where waiters race, balancing food orders high above their heads, with pained and confused looks on their faces.

Tony himself is the head waiter. A high-spirited, short, balding man, he shuffles quickly from table to table, sometimes mixing up the orders he delivers. But it doesn't seem to bother him or the diners—after all, everything tastes good here.

A large carafe of *Lambrusco Di Sorbara*, a sparkling, ruby-red wine with a dry, fresh flavor, lands on our table. Then Tony disappears to the far end of the room. Although hidden by rising steam, the constant clank of plates and the sizzle of grilling meat let us know that's where the kitchen is.

Starting this evening's feast is *tagliatelle e prosciutto*, strips of wide pasta in a cream and ham sauce, sprinkled with lots of grated *parmigiano* cheese. I enjoy every rich, gooey bite. Kevin has *tortellini ragu*, cheese-filled pasta ringlets smothered in a hearty sauce of tomatoes, three kinds of meat, vegetables, and red wine. An outstanding combination, according to Kevin.

For the second course, I opt for *lombatine alla parmigiano*—veal cutlets, pan-fried until golden brown then topped with chopped parsley, Parma ham, grated *parmigiano* cheese, and a dash of sweet Marsala wine. It tastes as wonderful as it sounds. Kevin tries *cotechino con lenticchie*, a large pork sausage served on a bed of lentils. The fresh beans are a great complement to the lightly spiced meat.

For dessert, we order *frutta* (fruit), and Tony places a full bowl on our table. The apples, oranges, figs, and grapes cascading down the side are beautiful enough for a still-life. We pay only for what we eat.

The cool evening air slaps our faces as we leave Tony's busy world behind. We turn back for a last look—hungry diners are waiting in line for a taste of Bologna's best.

Trattoria Anna Maria

Vicolo De Facchini, 4
Bologna
Phone: 236-615
Hours: noon-2:30pm, 7:30pm-11:30pm. Closed
   Monday.
Cover charge: 2,500 lire/person. No service charge.
Cost of our meal: 46,500 lire
Wheel chair negotiable. &

Barely four-feet, ten-inches tall, Anna Maria, owner of
her namesake *trattoria*, is a ball of fire. Although aid-
ed by a waiter, she's in full command of the large, airy
dining room—taking orders, serving food, and even
cleaning tables. She never misses a beat or a request
from her customers.

   This eatery, hidden in an alleyway in Bologna's center,
is big with the local artistic community. Autographed
photos of stage and opera stars and vintage musical in-
struments crowd the walls.

   On the first page of the menu is a note: "At this restaurant, we use only our own pasta," and it's signed bold-
ly by the *signora* herself. That's the type of disclaimer
Kevin and I enjoy challenging.

   I select *gnocchi alla rucola e pinoli*, fat potato dumplings smothered in a thick cheese/cream sauce and sprinkled with pine nuts. Kevin chooses *tortellini al
gorgonzola*, pasta ringlets stuffed with meat and topped
with a pungent, yet smooth, cheese sauce. We can tell
Anna Maria isn't fooling—her homemade pasta tastes
fresh and delicious.

   Naturally we have high expectations for the second
course, and Anna Maria doesn't let us down. My *braci-
ole di maiale*, an inch-thick pork chop, is cooked to

THE REGION OF
EMILIA-ROMAGNA

N↑

PIAZZA
VIII AGOSTO

VIA VENTURINI

VIA ALESANDRINI

VIA DELLE MOLINE

← CENTRO

ANNA MARIA

VIA MENTANA

VICOLO FACCHINI

RATTORIA ANNA MARIA

BOLOGNA

order and arrives hot and juicy. Kevin's *agnello al for-no*, oven-roasted lamb spiced with fresh oregano and garlic, receives his full attention. Crunchy potatoes accompany both dishes.

The house wine is worth more than a mention, too. A carafe of *Trebbianino*, pale gold and delicately dry, is a perfect addition to our meal.

Though many of the dishes at Trattoria Anna Maria are priced slightly higher than at other *trattorie*, her ample portions and unforgettable dishes make it worth every extra penny.

THE REGION OF
EMILIA – ROMAGNA

N ↑

VIA DELLA REPUBBLICA

BORGO TOMMASINI

VIA MAESTRI

DELLA ROSA ↳

PIAZZA
SAN LORENZO

 RATTORIA–OSTERIA DELLA ROSA

PARMA

Trattoria-Osteria Della Rosa

Borgo Giacomo Tommasini, 19
Parma
Phone: 238-941
Hours: noon-3:00pm, 7:30pm-11:00pm. Closed
  Sunday.
Cover charge: 1,000 lire/person. No service charge.
Cost of our meal: 33,000 lire
Wheel chair negotiable. &

Running east to west, the Via Della Repubblica, Parma's busiest boulevard, cuts the city into two different neighborhoods. To the north, trendy boutiques like Le Arte Decorative and expensive restaurants cater to Parma's young, well-dressed executives. To the south, the city is darker, more mysterious, and certainly more colorful. Second-hand stores crowd the alleyways. Old men, clad in three layers of flannel shirts stuffed under suit jackets, discuss politics in the park. The women of the area lean out apartment windows and talk across the alleys while keeping an eye on children playing below. In the heart of all this is Trattoria-Osteria Della Rosa.

As Kevin and I walk in, we see a glass counter holding tempting platters of fried peppers, roasted potatoes, and sliced, ripe tomatoes. In the corner of this room, a small television blares a soccer game—Milan is winning. The back room, bordered in sky-blue wainscoting, contains shiny, black lacquer chairs and bare tables.

As soon as we sit, a waiter approaches and recites the three *primi piatti* (the first course) while he sets our places. Kevin chooses *tortellini parmigiano*, cheese-filled pasta ringlets tossed in butter and plenty of *parmigiano* cheese—the pride of this city. The *penne e pomodoro*, long, cylindrical noodles topped with a fresh, chunky, tomato sauce, is for me.

Throughout dinner, locals wander in and out of the *trattoria*, ordering food directly from the counter and then carrying it to an empty table. Some customers leave their seats between courses to watch the game on TV.

Once our plates are wiped clean, the waiter returns to relate the three *secondi piatti* (the second course). We choose *vitello tonnato* (thin slices of tuna crowned with a dollop of creamy mayonnaise, lemon juice, and capers) and *arrosto di vitello*, a large veal cutlet charbroiled to juicy perfection. We also enjoy *piatto misto verdure*, a plate of cold vegetables (cauliflower, spinach, and green beans).

After we eat every bite and drink every drop of the house wine (a dry, white *Trebbiano Di Romagna*), we follow the other patrons to the front counter to pay our bill.

Although eating at Della Rosa is a lesson in listening (there is no written menu) and a test of our Italian (no one speaks English), it is genuine Parma life.

Trattoria Madonna

Via G.B. Borghesi, 3
Parma
Phone: 33-126
Hours: open daily noon-2:30pm, 6:30pm-10:30pm.
Cover charge: 1,500 lire/person. No service charge.
Cost of our meal: 35,000 lire
Wheel chair negotiable. &

From the outside, all there is to Trattoria Madonna is a hand-printed menu hanging from a window. But once we enter, we're overwhelmed by two five-foot oil paintings of the Madonna and Jesus staring serenely down on us. In a corner, a small shrine is complete with wax flowers and a statue of the Madonna draped in rosary beads.

One little room comprises both dining area and kitchen, separated by a long take-out counter. Customers unfamiliar with the day's specials are free to roam into the kitchen and see what's simmering on the stove, as long as they don't get underfoot.

There's no menu. The owner and chef, Giuseppina Orsi, a short, plump woman with a knack for Emilia-Romagna specialties, cooks two or three pasta and meat dishes every day. Her *lasagne* is a variation on the traditional version; she spreads ground veal and pine nuts between the layers of pasta and sauce. Even her *cannelloni*, those long, cheese-filled pasta tubes, have an added personal touch: finely chopped vegetables give a new texture to a delicious old standard.

The wine is *Lambrusco*, a sparkling red with a semi-dry flavor. Emilia-Romagna loves its carbonated wines, but for those who don't agree, Trattoria Madonna also offers beer.

THE REGION OF
EMILIA - ROMAGNA

N ↑

VIALE BOTTEGO

VIALE MENTANA

MADONNA ↘

VIA BORGHESI

VIA GARIBALDI

↓ CENTRO

TRATTORIA MADONNA

PARMA

For our second course, Kevin and I try the *signora's petto pollo con le noce*, a chicken breast sautéed with lots of onions, wine, pine nuts, and chunks of celery and carrots. We relish the multitude of different tastes and gobble up every juicy mouthful.

There's no dessert offered, but we relax with a cup of *espresso*. It's the best we've had yet, percolated on the stove in a small pot. We think it's a luxury to have freshly brewed Italian coffee, but at tiny Trattoria Madonna it's a necessity—they don't have room for a bulky *cappuccino* machine.

THE REGION OF
EMILIA-ROMAGNA

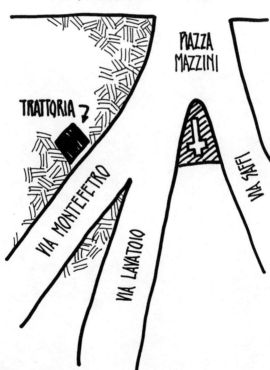

CENTRO

VIA GARIBALDI

N

VIA OCCIDENTALE

PIAZZA MAZZINI

TRATTORIA

VIA SAFFI

VIA MONTEFETRO

VIA LAVATOIO

 RATTORIA

RIMINI

Trattoria

Via Montefeltro, 19
Rimini
No phone.
Hours: noon-3:00pm, 7:00pm-10:30pm. Closed
    Sunday.
No cover charge. No service charge.
Cost of our meal: 21,000 lire
Wheel chair negotiable. &

This *trattoria*, located in the seaside resort of Rimini,
has no name and no phone. But this unpretentious spot
with its worn face is absolutely the best dining bargain
in northern Italy.

I pause for a moment at the door. The place is packed
with men, their shirt sleeves rolled up, concentrating
on big bowls of pasta—not a single woman diner.

I shrug and, as we enter, customers look curiously—
our camera bags and bad Italian immediately give us
away. A woman hurries past with plates of steaming
food and motions to the only vacant table. She and her
sister handle the dining room. Their mother and one
husband cook, while the second husband mans the bar.

Nothing matches in this place, from the battered, old
chairs to the silverware on the table. Brown, plastic
wainscoting lines the dining hall. There are no pictures
on the walls, just an occasional hat rack and a few old
clocks. At one table, elderly men, arms resting on the
backs of their chairs, cigarettes dangling from their
finger tips, are drinking small glass of *Campari* and
staring at the lunchtime customers.

Our waitress appears with a half-carafe of *Sangiovese*, a deep red wine from Forli, and a verbal list of
today's three entreés.

Obviously the *trattoria's* decor is no reflection on the food: my *pasta cici* is so good, I ask for the recipe. "Oh, it's easy," our waitress explains. "Water, olive oil, chickpeas, and fresh rosemary. After two hours, I add noodles." But as I slurp away, I'm convinced she's withholding a secret ingredient. Kevin's *tagliatelle con piselli*—bright yellow egg noodles in a cream sauce and lots of peas—is equally tasty.

Rimini is a large fishing port, tapping the nearby Adriatic for fresh seafood. Many *trattorie* boast *brodetto di pesce*—fish stew—and this mysterious, nameless diner offers an exceptional rendition. Several large pieces of eel, flounder, bass, mullet—plus whole sardines, crawfish, clams, and mussels—sit in a shallow bath of white wine, olive oil, and garlic. We need a second basket of bread just to soak up all the juice left behind.

Don't let the plain decor and male-dominated crowd stop you from trying this wonderful *trattoria*. No where else will you find a more congenial staff, true regional cooking, and rock-bottom prices. But remember, few tourists ever venture here, so treat it with respect—no Bermuda shorts or knee socks and sandals, please!

The Regions of Piedmont and Val D'Aosta

Although Piedmont and the politically annexed area Val D'Aosta boast landmarks like Mount Blanc, the Matterhorn, and miles of pristine Alpine country, most motoring Americans whisk through in a hurry to Venice, Florence, and Rome. But a visit to this northwest corner of Italy will convince you that Italian cuisine isn't just pasta and pizza.

The close proximity to France and Switzerland has greatly influenced the cooking habits of the area. Italians refer to the region's largest city, Turin, as "the most Italian city in France," since the food is more French than Italian. For a truer taste of Piedmont cooking, travelers should visit smaller cities like Alba, Mondovi, and Asti.

The region's prized ingredient is the white truffle—edible fungi found at the base of oak, willow, and hazelnut trees. Indigenous only to this part of the world, white truffles are added to everything from salads to *polenta*. Italians are so obsessed with them, they send dogs—with their keen sense of smell—to a school to be trained in proper mushroom-hunting technique. Harvest time, November-February, is the best time to visit, when the truffle is at its peak flavor.

The local cuisine relies heavily on warm, hearty soups, *polenta*, and roasted game—simple in style, but abundant in fresh flavor—to combat the harsh winters. A favorite appetizer is *bagna calda* ("hot bath"), a bubbling mixture of olive oil, chopped anchovies, lots of

VAL D'AOSTA

PIEDMONT

THE REGION OF

PIEDMONT AND VAL D'AOSTA

garlic, and truffle slices, all brought to the table in a pot placed over a small flame. Diners then swirl raw vegetables into the heavenly brew and, as the name implies, it instantly warms the entire body.

Another specialty is *fonduta*. Similar to Swiss fondue, the Italian version blends local *fontina* cheese, milk, butter, and egg yolks to form a thick porridge. Covered with chopped white truffles and served steaming hot, it's eaten as a first course in place of pasta, *risotto*, or *polenta*. Instead of dipping chunks of bread into a communal fondue pot, Italians prefer to eat every creamy mouthful of *fonduta* all by themselves.

Not every specialty is an adaption from the Swiss or French. *Grissini* (bread sticks) are a purely Italian invention. Although today they're made throughout the world, the thinnest and crunchiest still come from Piedmont, where a Torinese baker, Antonio Brunero, baked his first stick in 1679.

The area also produces exceptional red wines. The most common, *Barbera*, has a beautiful ruby color and can be drunk young. *Barolo*, another red, needs to age at least three years. And for those who love martinis, Piedmont is home to the best Italian vermouth.

THE REGION OF
PIEDMONT

N↑

CORSO VITTORIO EMANUELE II

STAZIONE
PORTA NUOVA

VIA NIZZA

VIA SALUZZO

DA FELICE

VIA BERTHOLLET

TRATTORIA DA FELICE

TURIN

Trattoria Da Felice

Via Saluzzo, 5
Turin (Region of Piedmont)
Phone: 650-5430
Hours: noon-2:30pm, 7:00pm-midnight. Closed
   Sunday.
Cover charge: 2,500 lire/person. No service charge.
Cost of our meal: 48,500 lire
Wheel chair negotiable. &

Trattoria Da Felice, like the city of Turin, is stylish and
contemporary. The large, bright, airy setting attracts
local business people and artists. Uniformed waiters at-
tend the two dozen tables adorned in crisp, peach cloths
and fresh-cut flowers. While the inside pulsates with
conversation and laughter, a set of French doors with
bare wood frames leads to a more intimate, candle-lit,
outside dining area.

   Kevin and I decide to sit inside, where the action is.
We order a carafe of *Boca*, dry and ruby red, with its
characteristic bouquet of violets, and carefully study
the extensive menu.

   I excitedly order *fonduta allo speck*, one of the tasti-
est regional dishes. *Fontina* cheese, milk, butter, and
egg yolks are carefully cooked in a double boiler to
avoid curdling, or, as the Italians say, *"impazzire"* ("to
go mad"). It's served very hot, topped with thin slices
of cured meat. It's unlike anything I've ever tried, and
I can't get enough of this creamy specialty, so I don't
even consider sharing with Kevin! Luckily, his *pappardelle alla boscaiola*, wide ribbon noodles with a
mushroom/cream sauce, is so flavorful, he's not interested in mine.

   About 10:00pm, a man dressed in second-hand

clothes covered with political and humorous buttons explodes into the room and shouts, *"Buona sera!"* He plays a lively folk song on his accordion, and many patrons sing along—even the chef joins the chorus. When he's finished, he gathers spare change from several diners, and then, as quickly as he arrived, he's gone. Oddly, we see him again several weeks later in Milan, wearing the same crazy clothes and singing the same song. And we thought writing guidebooks was a strange way to make a living!

Once the dining room returns to normal, our waiter delivers our second course. I have *salmone ai ferri* (grilled salmon). The fish is so large, it hangs over my plate. Kevin enjoys *capretto al forno*, kid (lamb) stuffed with stalks of fresh rosemary, thyme, and oregano, then roasted. For a final touch, we order *ciliege al barolo*— fresh cherries in red wine.

We're so full, we nearly roll out the door. At 11:00pm, the *trattoria* is far from closing.

Trattoria Alba

Via Bava, 2
Turin (Region of Piedmont)
Phone: 832-914
Hours: noon-3:00pm, 7:00pm-11:00pm. Closed
  Wednesday.
Cover charge: 1,500 lire/person. No service charge.
Cost of our meal: 21,000 lire
Wheel chair negotiable. ♿

Trattoria Alba, near the University of Torino, is a true family-run operation. Mom and Dad cover the front counter—pouring drinks, greeting customers, and watching the till. Their sons cook, and their daughters serve. Though the family is lovely, the featured attraction at Trattoria Alba is Pepe, the family's Scottish terrier. He roams politely among the patrons seated at red-checkered table tops, looking for a scratch behind his ears.

Alba is always packed. Diners don't come for the decor—huge water pipes run the length of the ceiling, plastic chandeliers illuminate the room, and "Dogs Playing Pool" paintings adorn the wall. But what Alba lacks in chic, it makes up for in attractively priced, good food.

Seated in the midst of the crowd, we say hello to Pepe and Francesca takes our order. Kevin has *ravioli alla piedmontese*, pasta pockets stuffed with meat and spinach, served with tomato sauce. I try *cappelletti in brodo*, Piedmont's version of *tortellini*. These tiny ringlets of meat-stuffed pasta float in a bowl of steaming chicken broth (*brodo*). Of course, we order a half-carafe of *Barbera*, red and dry.

The waitresses, each dressed in baggy, faded Levi's,

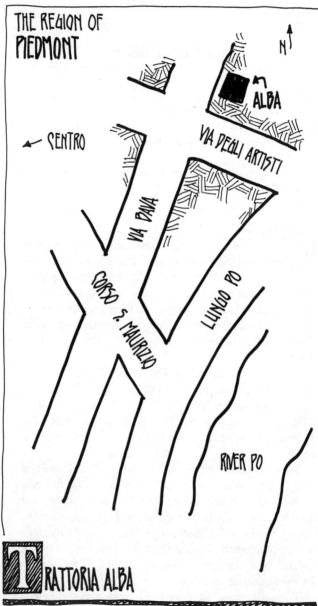

THE REGION OF
PIEDMONT

N

ALBA

← CENTRO

VIA DEGLI ARTISTI

VIA DANA

CORSO S. MAURIZIO

LUNGO PO

RIVER PO

TRATTORIA ALBA

TURIN

meander in and out of the back room, shouting their orders diner-style to the kitchen. The girls slide past one another with piping hot plates of food, instinctively aware of beloved Pepe at all times, never stepping on his paws.

Alba's menu contains a wide variety of pork, veal chops, stews, and grilled seafood. Kevin's *pollo arrosto*, a tender chicken leg roasted in wine and vegetables, is delicious. After seeing huge bowls of steamed mussels whisk by, I know what I want—*cozze al marinara*, a pile of sweet shellfish soaked in a bath of tomatoes, white wine, and garlic. When I'm finished, I use the largest shell as a spoon and slurp up all the juice left in my bowl.

After lunch, we say goodbye to Pepe and venture back into the noisy streets of Turin in search of dinner—only four hours away.

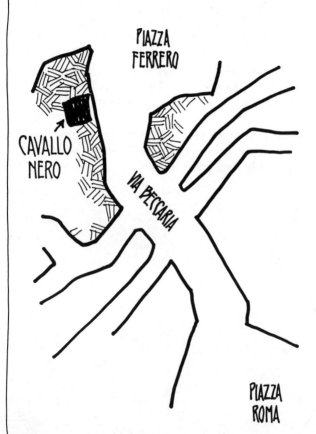

THE REGION OF
PIEDMONT

N

PIAZZA
FERRERO

CAVALLO
NERO

VIA BECCARIA

PIAZZA
ROMA

RATTORIA CAVALLO NERO

MONDOVI

Trattoria Cavallo Nero

Via Beccaria, 55
Mondovi (Region of Piedmont)
Phone: 43-573
Hours: noon-2:30pm, 7:00pm-11:00pm. Closed
  Monday.
Cover charge: 2,000 lire/person. No service charge.
Cost of our meal: 31,000 lire
Wheel chair negotiable. &

Since the city of Mondovi, located in southern Piedmont, is famous for its fine red wine, Kevin and I eagerly order a half-bottle of *Dolcetto Di Dogliani* the
moment we take our seats at Trattoria Cavallo Nero.
It's a departure from our usual half-carafe of house wine
routine, but even people traveling on a tight budget need
to splurge now and then. We savor the velvety, dry
flavor and ruby color through our first course of *penne
ragu*, long, cylindrical noodles covered with a robust
meat sauce, and *pasta forno*. Similar to *lasagna*, this
flat pasta is layered with creamy *fontina* cheese and
spiced veal, then baked until golden brown. Both are
wonderful mountain fare.

Situated on the corner of Piazza Ferrero, Cavallo
Nero's unobtrusive building is easy to miss. The inside,
though plain, is warm and inviting—low lights, linen
tablecloths, shelves filled with pottery, and pictures of
country scenes on the walls.

While we eat, the owner, Carla Olearo, roams among
her customers with a bread basket, depositing several
thick, crunchy breadsticks and rolls at each table. She
pays close attention to us—her only non-natives—and
slowly explains every dish, using hand gestures when
it's the only way to get us to understand.

For his second course, Kevin tries a local specialty, *rolata di coniglio*—rabbit fillets rolled tightly in herbs and baked in tomato sauce. It has a rich, hearty flavor. I order *rolata di pollo con funghi*—chicken breasts stuffed with ham and stalks of fresh rosemary, then rolled and roasted with wine and slices of Piedmont's fleshy mushrooms. We also try a local vegetable dish, *peperonata*—sweet yellow peppers, sliced black olives, and crushed tomatoes.

After lunch, we thank Carla for her kindness and applaud her innovative cooking. Back in the car, our conversation revolves around the richly textured food and smooth wine. We hope all of Piedmont is this good.

Gran San Bernardo

Via Martinet, 4
Aosta (Region of Val D'Aosta)
Phone: 40-042
Hours: 11:30am-1:30pm, 6:30pm-10:00pm. Closed
  Sunday.
Cover charge: 1,000 lire/person. No service charge.
Cost of our meal: 33,500 lire
Wheel chair negotiable. &

During our travels through Italy, Kevin and I learned an important lesson: at *trattorie*, there's no such thing as a "late lunch." All too often, we entered a restaurant just shy of 1:30pm and found the place empty and the waitress mopping up.

In the far northwest of Italy, close to the French border, we finally find an exception to the rule when we arrive at Gran San Bernardo about 1:30. As we expected, the eatery is nearly dead. Only two bearded men—philosopher types—sit at a corner table drinking *espresso*, too deep in conversation to notice our arrival. Already the chef and his family have retired from the open kitchen. "I guess they're closed," Kevin whispers, as we turn to leave.

"No, no, no," says the owner, Celeste Bianquin, as she rises from her chair. She points to a corner table, and we obey—in Italy, you should never refuse an invitation to eat. Besides, we're starving.

From a back cupboard, she pulls out a large piece of white paper and gently lays it across our table. Meanwhile, Celeste's daughter pours a carafe of red wine from the family bottle. The large glass flask of *Rosso Rubino*—a smooth local wine—is temporarily sealed with a soda-pop cap.

THE REGION OF
VAL D'AOSTA

N

PIAZZA
RONCAS

VIA MARTINET

APPLE TREES

GRAN SAN
BERNARDO

VIA XXVI FEBBRAIO

VIALE DELLA PACE

RAN SAN BERNARDO

AOSTA

Since our French is worse than our Italian, Celeste kindly relates the three *primi piatti* (first courses) in Italian. I choose *spaghetti pomodoro*, pasta topped with chunks of tomatoes and a dollop of sweet butter. Since this Alpine region is known for its warming soups, Kevin tries *minestrone*, a tasty combination of finely chopped vegetables and pasta noodles in chicken stock.

In the quiet of the afternoon, we examine San Bernardo's tiny interior. Devoid of pictures or paintings, the decor is clean and simple. The white stucco room has a low, cross-ribbed ceiling with hand-blown glass globes hanging above the eight tables.

For our second course, I feast on a wonderful *pollo arrosto* (half a chicken roasted in white wine and herbs), while Kevin has *costolette alla valdostana*, a breaded veal chop stuffed with *fontina* cheese and *prosciutto* ham then sautéed in butter—three delicate tastes, one great dish.

By the time we finish our meal, the men in the corner have progressed from *espresso* to *grappa*, a strong distilled spirit. Celeste thanks us as we leave, only this time she doesn't move from her chair. We understand— her steaming bowl of pasta is more important.

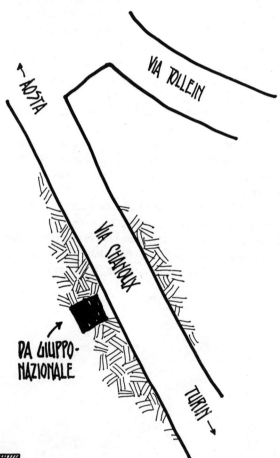

THE REGION OF
VAL D'AOSTA

N ↑

VIA TOLLEIN

↑ AOSTA

VIA CHANOUX

DA GIUPPO-
NAZIONALE

TURIN ↓

DA GIUPPO-NAZIONALE

CHATILLON

Da Giuppo-Nazionale

Via E. Chanoux, 162
Chatillon (Region of Val D'Aosta)
Phone: 62-79
Hours: noon-2:30pm, 7:00pm-10:30pm. Closed
   Sunday.
Cover charge: 2,000 lire/person. No service charge.
Cost of our meal: 34,500 lire
Wheel chair negotiable. &

In the village of Chatillon in the far northwest, we're
thrilled to find a place that looks promising: Da Giuppo-
Nazionale. Although the menu outside lists many
regional specialties, I peer in the door and spy a crowd
of locals gathered around a few worn sofas, drinking
wine. I sheepishly enter the room to investigate further,
fearing Da Giuppo-Nazionale is simply a bar. Immediately a waitress approaches. *"Manga?"* she asks, smiling
and pointing to a dining room behind two, swinging
bar doors. The decor instantly switches from beer mugs
to white linen and crystal goblets.

Kevin and I peruse the vast menu, discussing which
regional dishes we want to sample. The wine list is also
impressive, with a variety of Piedmont and Val D'Aosta vintages—*Spumanti, Barbera, Barbaresco,* and *Barolo.* We decide on a half-carafe of *Barbaresco,* with a
deep garnet color and a full, dry taste.

In the Alps, the local cuisine is hearty, to say the least.
By the time we finish our first course—*risotto valdostana* ("rice of the valley"), a creamy blend of rice
and *fontina* cheese, and *gnocchi di patate alla piedmontese,* a heaping bowl of potato dumplings with a sauce
of tomato, herbs, red wine, and veal—Kevin and I think
we can't eat another bite.

So we take a break and watch the events around us. The neighborhood bar patrons have become a little boisterous, acting out stories and telling jokes. One man stands on the couches, arms outstretched while he tells a story, his audience in rapt attention.

Our waitress approaches and addresses us in French. Normally I would think this strange, but Chatillon is a French name and only a few miles from the French border. She laughs as I order my next course in Italian. (Was she laughing at her confusion or my bad Italian?) I try *salsicetta al rosmarino*, a thick wheel of mild pork sausage skewered on a stick of rosemary then grilled brown and crispy. Kevin opts for *trota alle mandorle e nocciole*, fresh mountain trout basted with almond and hazelnut butter.

When we finish, we can't understand how the people of this valley can eat so much and stay so slim, but the walk back to our hotel, up steep streets and stairs, provides an answer.

The Regions of
Trentino-Alto Adige &
Friuli-Venezia Giulia

Although the area of Veneto separates Trentino-Alto Adige and Friuli-Venezia Giulia, the two regions have more in common than their complicated names. Both are heavily wooded and sharply punctuated by the Dolomite mountains. Life in each region is simple and unhurried. Most importantly, though, each region belonged to another country before World War I—the former to Bavaria, the latter to Austria.

Neighboring Germany and Austria have greatly influenced these regions in architecture and language. The bright green window shutters of central Italy are replaced by bare wood in Trentino and Friuli. Time-worn farmhouses change to A-frame structures. Even farmers' hats go from berets to yodeler's caps. Driving in Italy's far north presents a challenge, too—most road signs are in German.

The local cuisines, though different from each other, are vastly different from the rest of Italy. Heavy, doughy entrees are popular in these cold areas. Chefs concoct many variations on the dumpling, reflecting Tyrolean origins. In Trentino, for example, *ravioli* becomes *canederli*—bread dumplings usually served with a little olive oil.

In Friuli, eggs are very popular and used in *frittata*, an Italian omelette. They also add potatoes to their diet with *frico*, a pancake of sliced potatoes, *fontina* cheese, and onions, served hot, thin, and crisp.

Soups are a major staple, often simple and based on

TRENTINO

FRIULI

THE REGION OF

RENTINO and FRIULI

bread and *polenta*. Two favorites in both areas are *minestra d'orzo* (ham stock and lots of barley) and *minestra di farina tostata* (toasted flour soup).

The most popular meat is *speck*—pork roasted intermittently, two to three hours at a time, over a period of several months. Trentinos and Friulians say their high altitude and cold climate gives the meat a stronger flavor. Passirin Valley residents are considered master *speck*-makers. You'll also find sausage everywhere. In Italian, it's *salsiccia*; in German, it's *wurst*.

In eastern Friuli, apple trees cover the countryside, making *strudel*—fruit-filled pastry—the top dessert.

Locals often prefer beer over wine. *Forst*, a light pilsner, is the beer most available. For those who insist on the grape, *Traminer*, a fruity white wine, is the *vin* of the regions.

The melding of language, culture, and cuisine, coupled with spectacular Alpine scenery, makes Trentino and Friuli unlike any other part of Italy. It's an unforgettable addition to a traveler's agenda.

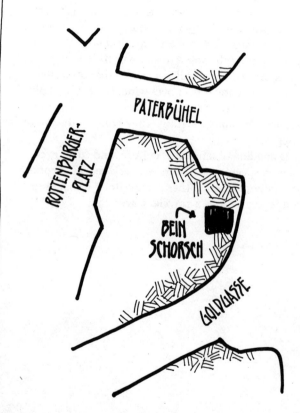

THE REGION OF
TRENTINO – ALTO ADIGE

N↑

PATERBÜHEL

ROTENBURGER-PLATZ

BEIN SCHORSCH

GOLDGASSE

BEIN SCHORSCH

CALDARO

Bein Schorsch

Goldgasse, 4
Caldaro (Kaltern) (Region of Trentino-Alto Adige)
Phone: 962-681
Hours: noon-3:00pm, 7:00pm-midnight. Closed
  Monday.
No cover charge. No service charge.
Cost of our meal: 26,000 lire
Wheel chair negotiable. &

Today's journey through the Dolomite mountains has been one of the prettiest yet, filled with wide, lush valleys between towering, snow-capped peaks. By the time Kevin and I reach Caldaro (or Kaltern, if you're of Austrian heritage), we're a little confused. Although we're miles from the Austrian border, the flavor of the area turns Alpine, with steep, A-frame houses and farmers wearing yodeler's caps.

At twilight, we stroll down the quiet, vineyard-lined country road to Caldaro's main square in search of dinner. Restaurants blanket the city center, but it's standing room only at Bein Schorsch. Following our *Trattoria* Rule #1— "Locals know the best places" —we push inside.

A strange mix of American blues, German folk songs, and Italian pop plays loudly on the sound system as we inch toward the bar. A young barmaid, no more than 15, addresses us in German, but before we can reply, she tries again in Italian. Kevin points to the tap.

Understanding, she draws two frosty mugs of *Forst*, a pale pilsner beer, and then hands us a menu while we wait for a table. It's written in German, but we're able to decipher a few things like *spaghetti mit tomatensauce*.

Noticing our trouble, the barmaid leaves her post to translate it into Italian. When she's stumped by a word, she yells to the grill chef, a young man with dark, curly hair and a mass of gold chains around his neck, who looks like he belongs in a Roman pizzeria rather than an Alpine *trattoria*. The fragrant aroma of grilled sausage fills the room as he moves the links across the hot, smoky surface. When he pulls a large, oven-browned hunk of meat out of a caldron, I shout "What is it?" He slices a sample, extending it on a long fork. We thank him and pop the tender, salty pork in our mouths—it's a super appetizer.

In the dining area next door, six tables fill one tiny room. We wiggle our way into our seats, practically falling in our neighbor's lap. No one minds though, since the beer flows freely, and strangers quickly become friends.

We skip the pizza and pasta tonight and eat what everyone else is having—*schweinsstelzen mit pommes frites und gemischten salat*, a pork thigh the size of a basketball, with french fries and a salad. The meat is surrounded by a crunchy layer of fat. Our fellow dinner companions watch curiously and laugh as we try to cut pounds of pork away from the center bone. Not too many tourists make it to Bein Schorsch, so tonight we're the talk of the restaurant.

By the time we leave, everyone knows we're the visiting Americans. They all shout farewells in German and Italian, and encourage us to return. We know we will.

Dolomiten

Via Haller, 4
Merano (Region of Trentino-Alto Adige)
Phone: 36-377
Hours: noon-3:00pm, 7:00pm-11:00pm. Closed
  Wednesday.
No cover charge. No service charge.
Cost of our meal: 41,000 lire
Not wheel chair negotiable.

The mountainous spa city of Merano is fewer than 30
miles from the Austrian border. Local food is unique—
neither Italian nor Austrian but Tyrolean, with lots of
doughy dumplings, thick *polenta*, and hearty soups.
Wanting to sample some true regional cuisine, we take
the suggestion of a life-long Alpine resident and head
for Dolomiten in the city center, near the Stein Museum.

The dwarfed entrance is deceiving. The restaurant is
actually deep and sprawling, with plenty of dark al-
coves. No one greets us at the door, so we follow the
aroma of sausage down a long hallway, ending up in
front of the kitchen, poorly located in the line of traffic.
Waiters, dressed in traditional Alpine costumes, elbow
us out of the way as they whisk past with plates of hot
food. It's Sunday, and it seems everyone in town is hungry for Dolomiten's dazzling entrees.

We quickly move to the rear dining area, a large room
with wood benches and tables and sun-filled windows
overlooking a vine-covered patio. The menu is written
in German, translated into Italian, and offers all the
Tyrolean specialties we're eager to try.

To get us into the Alpine spirit, we order two large
mugs of Italian beer—*Nastro Azzurro*, a light pilsner
with a slightly sweet after-taste. The cold brew is just

THE REGION OF
TRENTINO – ALTO ADIGE

N ↑

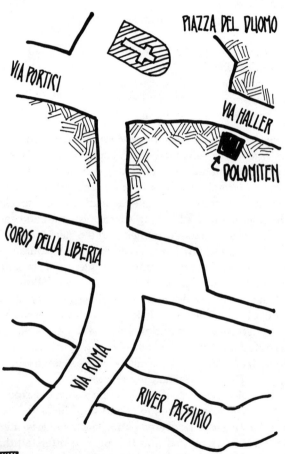

PIAZZA DEL DUOMO

VIA PORTICI

VIA HALLER

DOLOMITEN

COROS DELLA LIBERTA

VIA ROMA

RIVER PASSIRIO

 DOLOMITEN

MERANO

what we need to whet our appetites for the first course, *canederli di speck*. These plump dumplings made from bread and potatoes are similar to *gnocchi* but topped with chopped *speck* meat and a drizzle of olive oil.

The restaurant continues to buzz with German tourists in a feeding frenzy. We don't want to be left out, so we order *polenta con funghi e salsiccia alla griglia*, two long, thin pork sausages with sautéed mushrooms and slices of *polenta*. The corn meal mixture is crunchy on the outside, moist and flavorful inside.

After lunch, we sit out on the terrace to finish our beer. Besides, we're so full, we're afraid to move.

THE REGION OF
FRIULI-VENEZIA GIULIA

N ↑

VIALE VENEZIA

PIAZZA
LE XXVI LUGLIO

VIALE PUOPO

CENTRO →

PIAZZA LE CELLA

VIALE DELLE FERRIERE

AL CAVALLINO

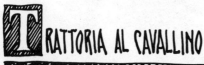

T RATTORIA AL CAVALLINO

UDINE

Trattoria Al Cavallino

Piazza le Cella, 27
Udine (Region of Friuli-Venezia Giulia)
Phone: 25-907
Hours: noon-2:00pm, 7:00pm-11:00pm. Closed
  Monday.
Cover charge: 1,500 lire/person. No service charge.
Cost of our meal: 32,000 lire
Not wheel chair negotiable.

Three outside influences—the Roman Catholic Patri-
arch of Aquileia, the conquering Venetians, and
Austria—have all ruled the city of Udine sometime
during the past 800 years. These influences have altered
and shaped Udine into a city neither Austrian nor typi-
cally Italian, but uniquely Friulian.

Trattoria Al Cavallino, in the busy Piazza le Cella,
less than a mile from the city center, is a quiet, fashiona-
ble dining spot popular with the local business crowd.
Many customers have been patronizing the *trattoria* for
years—they know all the waitresses and always sit at
the same tables. Polished teak wood abounds, from the
doors and moldings to a circular bench along the
perimeter of the dining room. Soft, recessed lighting
and pink table linens add to the gentle ambiance.

We first order a carafe of *Traminer*, then sit back and
sip the fruity, white wine. The largely mountainous area
of Friuli is known for warming soups, so we put Al
Cavallino to the test. I order *orzo e fagioli*, a thick barley
and bean soup with a base of tomatoes and ham. Kevin
tries something simpler—*consomme all'uovo*. Although
the recipe sounds effortless—clear chicken broth and
a raw egg—it's important that the consomme be flavorful and made from lean meat. Kevin drinks most of the

broth until just the right moment, then breaks the egg yolk and sops up the remaining mixture with a hunk of bread.

For our second course, Kevin orders *cotoletta alla valdostana*, a breaded veal cutlet stuffed with creamy *fontina* cheese and *speck*, the local smoked meat. I choose from a long list of fresh seafood. Tonight it's *zuppa di cozze vongole*, a large caldron of clams and mussels. Their salty bath water is a fragrant combination of herbs, garlic, parsley, and white wine.

Pushing away our now vacant plates, we bask in Al Cavallino's peaceful setting and entertain thoughts of another meal there—at the same table, of course.

El Corral

Via Guspergo, 8
Cividale (Region of Friuli-Venezia Giulia)
Phone: 733-174
Hours: 12:30pm-2:30pm, 7:00pm-10:00pm. Closed
  Monday and from November to spring.
Cover charge: 1,500 lire/person. No service charge.
Cost of our meal: 23,500 lire
Wheel chair negotiable. &

On a tip that there's a *trattoria* serving the cuisine of
Friuli, we turn off the highway from Cividale to the Yu-
goslavian border and soon find ourselves lost in a maze
of single-lane roads that connect one farmhouse to the
next. My stomach growls as we search for El Corral
among cornfields and vineyards. At first we're not
concerned—the sun is shining, and to the north, Dolomite foothills radiate a purple hue, their snow-capped
peaks spiraling into a cloudless sky.

   We agree to try one more route before giving up and
going hungry. Behind a corral of horses, we find a gravel
parking lot circling a large, two-story building. There's
no sign, but a glance through ground floor windows
reveals tables, chairs, and wine glasses. We found it!

   An array of barnyard animals—chickens, ducks,
geese—squawk and flutter at our feet as we walk
around the courtyard entrance. The dining area is new
(added to the end of the farmhouse) but stark—eight
picnic tables dressed in red wool blankets and a bar
made from uncut logs. Adding to our warmth and com-
fort on this chilly day, sunlight floods the room through
French doors running the length of one wall.

   Before ordering lunch, I ask the waitress to point the
way to the bathroom. It's outside, next to the barn and

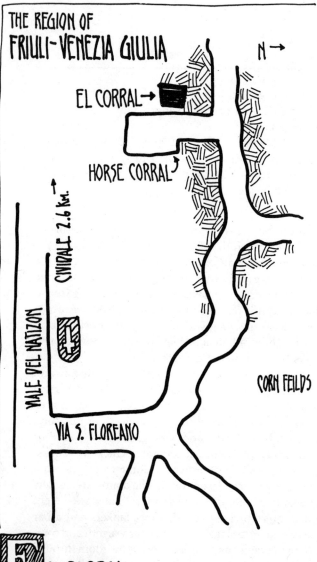

THE REGION OF
FRIULI-VENEZIA GIULIA

N →

EL CORRAL →

HORSE CORRAL

CIVIDALE 2.6 km.

VIALE DEL NATION

CORN FEILDS

VIA S. FLOREANO

L CORRAL

CIVIDALE

a rusted, red tractor. I have to chase away a rooster to get in the door. He ruffles his feathers and crows his displeasure before reluctantly stepping aside.

The menu at El Corral is simple—three *primi* and three *secondi*, all neatly written on a wall poster. Kevin and I both indulge in *gnocchi*, plump potato dumplings covered with a thick, Hunter's Sauce of tomatoes, rabbit, and rosemary. To drink—*Refosco*, a bright red wine with a bitter, dry flavor.

Our main course is a departure from the usual meat and fish. Today, I order *frico con patate*, a potato and *fontina* cheese pancake, pan-fried and served crispy brown and hot. Kevin has *frittata con le erbe*, an herb omelette. Sharing, we both enjoy this farm-fresh fare.

After lunch, we linger outside and listen to the sounds of the country: distant dogs bark, chasing a group of ducks; a tractor hums, cutting down corn stalks golden and dry from the late autumn sun. The drive back to the main highway is much easier with our stomachs full of rich, El Corral cooking.

THE REGION OF
FRIULI-VENEZIA GIULIA

N ↑

CIVIDALE 1.5 KM. ↑

554

ALLA FRASCHETTA ↗

↙ CEMETERY

← UDINE

ALLA FRASCHETTA
CIVIDALE

Alla Fraschetta

Via Scrutto, 66
Cividale (Region of Friuli-Venezia Giulia)
Phone: 723-382
Hours: noon-3:00pm, 7:00pm-10:00pm. Closed in
   winter and at the whim of owner.
Cover charge: 1,500 lire/person. No service charge.
Cost of our meal: 27,000 lire
Wheel chair negotiable. &

On the road from Udine to Cividale, Kevin spies a
cemetery with a black and pink stone building gracing
the entrance. He stops the car to take photos. Knowing
this usually becomes a long visit, I hop out to investigate the area, and that's when I see the hand-written
sign posted on the highway: "ALLA FRASCHETTA—*i
piatti tipici del Friuli*" ("the typical dishes of Friuli").
An arrow points to a tiny roadside stand bordered in
the back by vineyards and in the front by a large peb-
ble parking lot.

I pull Kevin in for a look. "Just for a *caffè* (strong
Italian coffee)," I coax. We approach slowly, not sure
what to think of this makeshift diner. The room is partially open—bamboo shades on two sides and a pull-
down fourth wall. Three long tables rest on a platform,
where three locals—two ladies and an elderly
gentleman—quietly eat bowls of pasta. Out front,
there's a bar with a few torn leather stools. A half-dozen
picnic tables are spread under a line of shade trees
outside.

The *signora*, a diminutive woman with short brown
hair and blue nails (tinted from the grape harvest),
enters from behind a beaded curtain to the kitchen.
Though she doesn't speak English, she is eager to talk,

her eyes widening with every animated gesture.

We skip the coffee and take a seat among the locals, now enjoying plates of *trippa* (tripe). With a fork in hand, we're ready for some authentic regional fare.

I start with *minestrone con orzo*, a warming bowl of vegetable soup with plenty of locally grown barley. Kevin has *frico con polenta*, a Friuli staple of pan-fried potato and *fontina* cheese pancake. Accompanying it is a small portion of *polenta*, a creamy, porridge-like mixture of maize and water, cooked slowly.

Our energetic chef/hostess also delivers a half-carafe of *Rosato Di Cividale*, the area's most popular red wine, deliciously light and refreshing. Next from her kitchen comes *fagioli con salsiccia*, a heaping platter of thin pork sausages on a bed of sautéed white beans and onions.

When we hand the *signora* money for the bill, she asks, "How do you say 'change' in English?" She watches my mouth form the word and tries to imitate me. Then she slides our lire back to Kevin. "American change—that's what I want. Do you have any?"

"No," we tell her. "Only lire."

"Maybe next time," she says, smiling as she scoops our money off the counter. And maybe next time, I'll look forward to another great meal when Kevin stops to take pictures.

The Regions of
Umbria and The Marches

Umbria and The Marches are my favorite regions in Italy. There's a peaceful simplicity to the land, a graceful nature to the people, and some of the best-tasting food anywhere. The two regions are comprised of remote hilltowns and deep, rich valleys nestled in the middle of Italy. Centuries ago, this central location became a melting pot of settlers from all over—Etruscans and Picenes from the east, Latins from the west, and Sabines and Samanites from the south.

Cultural differences resulted in fascinating variations on the same regional dish. Like mountain food everywhere, it's hearty fare, and here that means lot of meat and pasta. Hills covered with wild herbs and woods thick with acorn-laden oaks provide an unusual diet for the #1 industry—pigs. The best come from the land around Norcia, which gives us the Italian word *norcino* (butcher). With this in mind, it's no surprise that *porchetta*—roast suckling pig—is the most popular specialty, though its preparation differs from village to village.

The region's hard-working, mostly poor villagers waste nothing. They use the pig's liver to make sausage spiced with garlic, pepper, and coriander—*mazzafegati*. Wheat is another major product of the area, supplying *trattoria* tables with pasta dishes like *rigatoni alla norcina*—large, ribbed noodles with ground pork sausage.

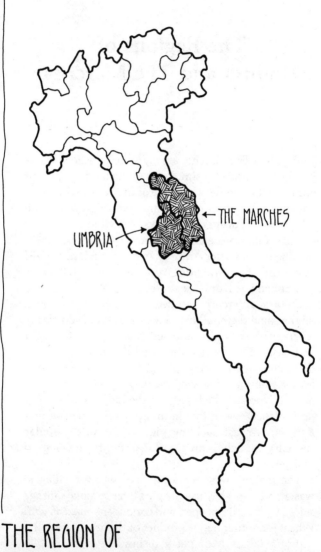

UMBRIA

THE MARCHES

THE REGION OF

MBRIA AND THE MARCHES

Umbria has truffles, too, only they're black and not as coveted as the prized (and expensive) white truffles from Piedmont. Yet Umbrian truffles are delicious. Try them in *spaghetti al tartufo nero* (pasta with black mushrooms).

The coastal towns provide the region with plenty of fish. A favorite way to prepare the fresh catch is simply to throw it into a hot fire. When the fish is completely charred, it's removed from the flame, and the burned scales are scraped off, leaving moist, tender meat inside to be seasoned with oil and spices. This unusual practice is called *pescati carbonaretti*.

The best wine, *Orvieto*, from the city of the same name, is dry with a slightly bitter aftertaste. A regional favorite, it's exported to many countries.

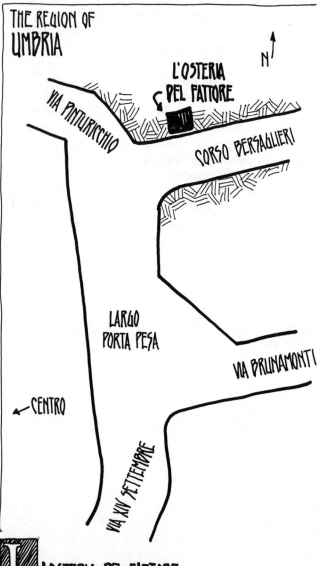

THE REGION OF
UMBRIA

N

L'OSTERIA
DEL FATTORE

VIA PINTURICCHIO

CORSO BERSAGLIERI

LARGO
PORTA PESA

VIA BRUNAMONTI

← CENTRO

VIA XIV SETTEMBRE

 L'OSTERIA DEL FATTORE

PERUGIA

L'Osteria Del Fattore

Corso Bersaglieri, 26
Perugia (Region of Umbria)
Phone: 25-864
Hours: noon-2:30pm, 7:00pm-11:30pm. Closed
   Sunday.
No cover charge. No service charge.
Cost of our meal: 40,000 lire
Not wheel chair negotiable.

Once an Etruscan stronghold, the walled hilltop city of
Perugia has moved comfortably into the 20th century
by placing its ancient history in modern settings. One
example: L'Osteria Del Fattore, a contemporary urban
trattoria offering centuries-old regional fare.

The recently renovated interior has an Asian feel.
Black lacquer furniture, spotlights bouncing off white
walls, a circular bar, and red linen accents make this
a high-fashion retreat.

As we take our seats, we're greeted by a basket of
chewy, pita-type bread—homemade and hot from the
oven. Although Del Fattore offers several inexpensive
regional wines, we pick a liter of the house wine—an
even less costly, local Perugian product, similar to *Colli Del Trasimeno*—straw yellow in color, with a well-
balanced bouquet.

For starters, Kevin and I choose *tagliatelle in salsa
tartufata*, broad pasta noodles with Umbria's famous
"wild black mushroom sauce." Each *trattoria* in this
region creates its own black mushroom sauce, and Del
Fattore's recipe combines lots of chopped garlic, parsley, olive oil, and truffles. The deep, woody flavor is
addictive.

Petti di pollo in salsa rosa is my second course selection. The chicken fillets, poached in white wine then covered with a creamy tomato puree, is wonderful; and so is Kevin's *agnello a scottadito*, seasoned lamb chops grilled to perfection. For our vegetable, we try an unfamiliar specialty—*gratinati*, slices of tomatoes, peppers, and eggplant sprinkled with bread crumbs and *parmigiano* cheese then baked until golden.

L'Osteria Del Fattore offers only the freshest product, a taste difference we can immediately appreciate. And unlike many *trattoria*, it includes the cover charge and service charge in the price of the entrées—a real help to budget-conscious travelers.

Pozzo Della Mensa

Via Pozzo della Mensa, 11
Assisi (Region of Umbria)
Phone: 816-247
Hours: noon-2:30pm, 7:00pm-11:00pm. Closed
   Wednesday.
Cover charge: 2,500 lire/person. No service charge.
Cost of our meal: 50,500 lire
Wheel chair negotiable. &

Pozzo Della Mensa is down a quiet alley lined with pink
stone buildings, not far from Assisi's Piazza del Com-
mune. Although the food is fresh and absolutely fantastic, the service is somewhat pretentious. A
stone-faced waiter, dressed in an Armani suit, ceremoni-
ously (and a bit unnecessarily) spoons out our pasta
at the table. The chef, decked-out in full white uniform,
occasionally strolls regally through the dining room.
His culinary awards, trophies, and photos of his accep-
tance speeches hang on the far wall. As if in awe, the
dining room is full of patrons speaking in hushed voices.

We ignore the pomp and circumstance and turn our
attention to truly important matters: the pasta on the
table, steaming hot and demanding consumption! Mine
is *ravioli con pozzo*, the house specialty. These trian-
gles of pasta, filled with *ricotta* cheese and topped with
a smooth tomato/cream and chopped *pancetta* (bacon)
sauce, taste so fresh, I'm convinced they were made only
moments ago. Kevin's *tagliatelle alla norcina* is an Umbrian specialty of broad noodles, ground pork, and
cream. The smoky meat and rich sauce is another
winner.

To entertain ourselves between courses, we try to
think of ways to make the solemn waiter laugh, but in-

THE REGION OF
UMBRIA

N↑

PIAZZA
DEL COMUNE

VIA S. RUFINO

CORSO MAZZINI

VIA S. GABRIELE DELL' ADD.

VIA POZZO DELLA MENSA

POZZO
DELLA
MENSA

POZZO DELLA MENSA

ASSISI

stead we end up giggling uncontrollably. Perhaps the house wine is playing a hand in our silliness. The *Torre Bianco*, a dry white wine from the neighboring hilltown of Montefalco, flows easily.

We manage to control ourselves just as the next course arrives. My *filetto alle bacche rosa*, a veal fillet quickly grilled over a smoldering fire, is charred on the outside but moist and pink inside. Kevin takes a moment to inhale the intoxicating aroma of the chopped black truffles and garlic sauce atop his *scaloppine al tartufo nero*, veal fillets cooked in white wine.

Walking back to the hotel, Kevin and I agree that although Pozzo Della Mensa has certainly earned the right to be taken seriously, they really ought to lighten up just a bit.

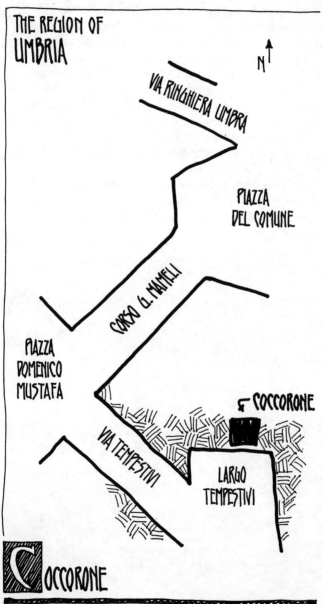

THE REGION OF
UMBRIA

N↑

VIA RINGHIERA UMBRA

PIAZZA
DEL COMUNE

CORSO G. MAMELI

PIAZZA
DOMENICO
MUSTAFA

COCCORONE

VIA TEMPESTIVI

LARGO
TEMPESTIVI

COCCORONE

MONTEFALCO

Coccorone

Largo Tempestivi
Montefalco (Region of Umbria)
Phone: 79-535
Hours: noon-2:30pm, 7:00pm-11:00pm. Closed
   Wednesday.
Cover charge: 2,000 lire/person. No service charge.
Cost of our meal: 53,000 lire
Not wheel chair negotiable.

As its name suggests, Montefalco is like a falcon perched
atop its nest. This small, walled Umbrian hilltown, set
amid olive groves and vineyards, offers sweeping vistas and a quiet, serene way of life, despite a sometimes
harsh climate. Indeed, the day we arrive the wind is
fierce, and there's no sound except the howling wind
and the flapping plastic drapes on the scaffolding in the
piazza.

The scent of a wood fire draws us to Coccorone. Situated in a converted residence, this *trattoria* retains a
homey, yet sophisticated, atmosphere. Several dining
rooms are connected by a series of brick archways, and
the ceiling is an exquisite labyrinth of dark, weathered,
centuries-old beams.

As we walk in, haze from a small hearth fills the
room. The *padrone*, embarrassed by this little mishap,
keeps opening the front door to air-out the room, but
that wakes his father dozing near the bar, and he closes
the door when his son's back is turned.

Coccorone doesn't offer liters of house wine, so we
order a bottle of *Rosso Montefalco*, a local wine with
a deep red color and velvety, dry taste. We begin the
meal with *stringozzi ai funghi*, string-like pasta tossed
in olive oil and chopped *porcini* mushrooms, and *pap-*

pardelle al sagrantino, wide ribbon noodles with red wine and *porcini* mushrooms. The rich, earthy flavors are fitting fare for such a stormy day.

The *signora* exits the kitchen with a platter of raw lamb chops and heads toward the small fire burning in the side dining room. Curious, I follow. She places the lamb on a rack directly over the smoldering embers. The meat sizzles and hisses while she attentively fans the hot coals to a brilliant red. When the lamb is done, she spreads a puree of black truffles, garlic, and parsley across each chop and serves immediately. This *agnello tartufato* is wonderful—seared outside, pink inside, and the black truffle sauce has a slightly spicy flavor.

A few hours later, we're back out in the wind, and there's still no one on the streets. As we walk toward the car, the aroma of Coccorone's fire fades, but certainly not the memory of such a great meal.

Trattoria La Palomba

Via Cipriano Manente, 16
Orvieto (Region of Umbria)
Phone: 43-395
Hours: noon-2:30pm, 7:00pm-10:30pm. Closed
 Wednesday.
Cover charge: 1,000 lire/person.
Service charge: 10%
Cost of our meal: 27,000 lire
Wheel chair negotiable. &

At the door of Trattoria La Palomba, located in Orvieto's historic quarter, stands a four-foot wooden Pinocchio covered with autographs of others who have told lies—even if their noses didn't grow because of them. This casual, out-of-the-way, hilltop cafe has been serving regional fare for nearly a century, so we're sure it's going to be good!

A blast of hot air hits us the moment we move the front curtain aside and enter the packed dining room. We squeeze into a corner table among boisterous locals dropping lit matches into empty carbonated-water bottles. They rock with laughter as the flame turns blue (from the remaining gas) and floats slowly down inside the glass.

The house wine arrives in an unmarked bottle. It's La Palomba's own brew, an unusually deep gold color with a stimulating dry flavor, and priced right for wine lovers.

Since I can't get enough of Umbria's black truffles, my first selection is easy—*umbrichelle tartufate*, thick, spaghetti-like pasta topped with black truffle sauce. Unlike the expensive white truffles of Piedmont, *tartufo nero* has a stronger, woodsier essence and is found inexpensively on *trattoria* menus. As an extra touch, the

THE REGION OF
UMBRIA

N ↑

CORSO CAVOUR

PIAZZA
DELLA
REPUBBLICA

VIA GARIBALDI

VIA C. MANENTE

↳ LA PALOMBA

TRATTORIA LA PALOMBA

ORVIETO

waiter produces a single black truffle and grates it over my pasta. Like a child watching a magic trick, I'm delighted! Kevin orders the house specialty—*spaghetti P.C.*, pasta in a light sauce of tomatoes and sliced artichokes.

For our second course, we share *salsicce*, several fat, spicy pork sausages sliced down the center, then grilled until crisp, and a plate of *insalata pomodoro*, sweet, vine-ripened tomatoes.

By the time we finish dinner, it's close to 11:00pm and the place is nearly empty. While one waiter sets the table for the kitchen crew's supper, another steps outside and shouts to the empty streets, *"Chiuso!"* ("We're closed!") After four hours on his feet, he still has a sense of humor—and that, plus great food, makes Trattoria La Palomba worth visiting.

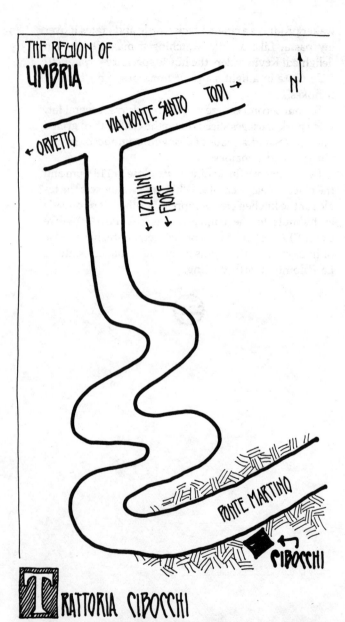

Trattoria Cibocchi

Ponte Martino, 67
Todi (Region of Umbria)
Phone: 882-949
Hours: 12:30pm-3:00pm, 7:30pm-11:30pm. Closed Friday.
Cover charge: 1,500 lire/person. No service charge.
Cost of our meal: 39,000 lire
Wheel chair negotiable. &

Trattoria Cibocchi is down a windy, bumpy country road less than a mile from the walled Etruscan city of Todi. We enter behind two local construction workers carrying their own wine, concealed in brown paper. Through the beaded, main entrance, the spacious dining room has large windows framing the Umbrian hills, towering cypress trees, and vineyards. Adjacent to the dining area is a private room, where Grandpa eats his lunch while watching an American soap opera dubbed in Italian.

Along with an ice-cold bottle of *Trebbiano*—Cibocchi's own clear, crisp white wine—comes a basket of thick, hot, pita-type bread. It's deliciously chewy, but there's a small charge for additional baskets.

The menu changes daily, offering simple pasta dishes and lots of freshly roasted fowl. Hooked on Umbria's black truffles, I order *ravioli con tartufo nero*, cheese-filled pasta pockets with chopped black truffles and fresh olive oil. Kevin starts with *fettuccine ragu*, long, flat noodles in a rich meat sauce.

A pass-through window allows me to watch the *signora* dish up lunch for this hungry crowd. A tall, unmarked bottle filled with sea-green olive oil stands next to the stove. It's another Cibocchi product and, before any dish leaves the kitchen, the *signora* drizzles the extra-virgin olive oil on top, like her signature on each creation.

For our second course, Kevin indulges in *lepre in salmi*, delicately seasoned pieces of rabbit simmered in olive oil, white wine, and whole green olives. I have *pollo in padella*, chicken cooked in a mild tomato and caper sauce.

A delightful change from city dining, Trattoria Cibocchi offers a chance to experience the Umbrian countryside and taste the bounty of its land.

Trattoria Del Leone

Via C. Battisti, 5
Urbino (Region of The Marches)
Phone: 329-894
Hours: noon-2:30pm, 7:00pm-11:00pm. Closed
  Sunday.
Cover charge: 2,000 lire/person. No service charge.
Cost of our meal: 44,000 lire
Not wheel chair negotiable.

Though the walled, hilltop city of Urbino in the northern Marches is an educational and cultural center that attracts artists and musicians from around the world, little has changed in the last 500 years. Mostly students, not tourists, roam the narrow streets lined with palaces. And while the Piazzale della Repubblica—the main square—draws the hip crowd in the evening, nearby Trattoria Del Leone still hosts their older, pipe-smoking professors.

The basement dining room is intimate, with a low, sloping ceiling, dim lighting, and copper pots hanging along the walls. The patrons seem to talk thoughtfully, discussing softly the paintings of Raphael and the buildings of Bramante, both natives of Urbino.

Kevin and I do some discussing or our own, like which pasta to order. My *spaghetti aglio olio* merits ample praise for its sautéed garlic and olive oil make-up, while Kevin's *risotto ai quattro formaggi*—chewy Arborio rice with four cheeses—disappears before I can test it. But Kevin kindly informs me the creamy sauce of *mozzarella*, *gruyere*, *fontina*, and *provolone* was a masterpiece.

Our beverage this evening is a carafe of *Colli Pesaresi*, a translucent red, dry wine with a delicate bouquet.

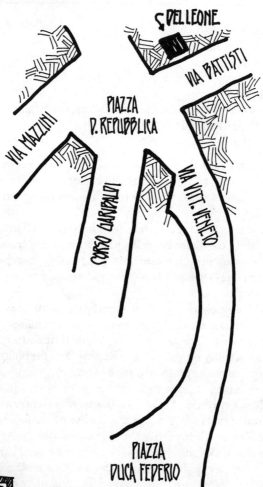

THE REGION OF
THE MARCHES

N ↑

ς DEL LEONE

VIA BATTISTI

VIA MAZZINI

PIAZZA
D. REPUBBLICA

CORSO GARIBALDI

VIA VITT. VENETO

PIAZZA
DUCA FEDERIO

 TRATTORIA DEL LEONE

URBINO

We manage to save a glass to share with our entrées: *fegato alla brace*, fresh liver quickly grilled over a smoldering fire, and *pollo arrosto con funghi*, chicken fillets simmered in red wine and *porcini* mushrooms. For dessert, we select another winner—*cicerchiata*, sweet honey cake sprinkled with chopped almonds and cinnamon.

Although it's raining hard when we leave Del Leone, the Piazzale della Repubblica is still hopping with students. We filter through the crowd until we find an empty spot on the brick wall sheltered from the rain, and watch the action.

THE REGION OF
THE MARCHES

N ↑

LA COMETA

VIA G. DA MONTEFELTRO

VIA DEL SANGUE

VIA PIANSEVERO

↓ CENTRO

 RATTORIA LA COMETA

URBINO

Trattoria La Cometa

Via Guido da Montefeltro, 7
Urbino (Region of The Marches)
Phone: 38-606
Hours: noon-3:00pm, 7:00pm-10:30pm. Closed
  Sunday.
Cover charge: 2,000 lire/person. No service charge.
Cost of our meal: 38,000 lire
Wheel chair negotiable. &

Like the city of Urbino, Trattoria La Cometa is a serene,
gentle hideaway. Located less than a mile from the
historic center, this quaint eatery has two separate
dining areas: a casual pizzeria with small, round patio
tables and an elegant room with linen, crystal, and
black-tied waiters. Rejecting the tempting idea of pizza, we sit in the fancy room.

A carafe of *Verdicchio*, a local dry white wine,
awakens our palates to the imaginative, mountain cuisine La Cometa promises to deliver.

Tonight I start with *stracciatella* (egg soup). Origi-
nally from Rome, this hot mixture of whisked egg,
chicken broth, bread crumbs, and grated *parmigiano*
cheese was quickly adopted in all areas of Italy. I savor
its silky smooth texture and unique flavor as much as
Kevin loves his *paglia e fieno* ("straw and hay"). This
famous pasta dish is a combination of two types of
matchstick-thin noodles: spinach and egg. Several
popular sauces for it include mushrooms and olive oil,
ham and cream, or Kevin's choice—fresh tomatoes. The
delicate pasta seems to melt away, leaving him wanting
more.

Perhaps a little out-of-place in La Cometa's swank
decor is a 19-inch color television perched in the cor-

ner. While we dine, we're entertained by Walt Disney's "Pinocchio" dubbed in Italian. The dining room grows quiet when the little puppet has his tearful reunion with Gepetto.

For our main course, we unanimously vote for *coniglio in porchetta*, the region's favorite specialty. Translated, it means, "rabbit cooked like a suckling pig," referring to fennel, the herb traditionally used with suckling pig. Rosemary, garlic, and ham are also added to the rabbit's tasty stuffing. It's served golden brown with a fine white wine sauce.

The country cuisine offered at La Cometa is lovingly prepared and served—and the movie is free.

La Tana Di Pecoz

Corso Mazzini, 277
Ascoli Piceno (Region of The Marches)
Phone: 256-760
Hours: noon-2:00pm, 7:00pm-11:00pm. Closed
   Wednesday.
Cover charge: 2,500 lire/person. No service charge.
Cost of our meal: 37,000 lire
Wheel chair negotiable. &

In the center of Ascoli Piceno is the Piazza Del Popolo, a huge, marble square bordered by *palazzi* (palaces) and a porticoed galleria. At dusk, locals descend upon this aptly named "People's Square" for the *passeggiata* (promenading). Youths lounge outside the Church of St. Francis, leaning against the stone walls. Old men crowd the outlying cafes, while well-dressed couples wheeling baby carriages tour the massive plaza.

Shortly after the church bells signal 7:00pm, residents filter from side streets and alleyways to their favorite *trattorie*. We try to beat the crowd, but when we enter La Tana Di Pecoz, only one empty table is left. We grab it. The dining room is quietly elegant, with pale yellow, stucco walls and a high, cross-ribbed ceiling. The place settings are simple, with long-stemmed wine goblets and no salt and pepper.

Delivering a carafe of *Rosso Piceno*, a wine that's dark, ruby-red, robust, and dry, the owner stays to chat. "I know very little English," he says in Italian. Then he cups his hands over his ears as though he's wearing headphones and announces in English: "Ladies and gentlemen—Jim Morrison and The Doors!" After his droll imitation, he rocks back and forth to an imaginary beat while we break up with laughter.

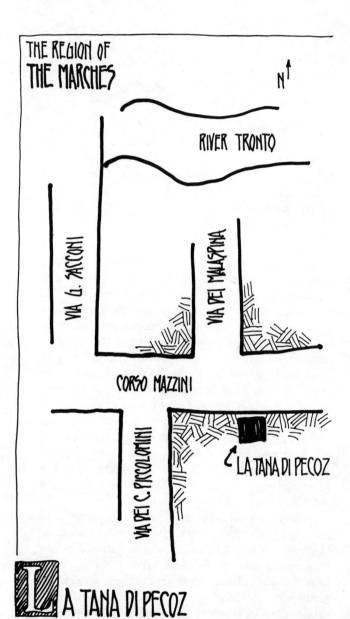

THE REGION OF
THE MARCHES

N↑

RIVER TRONTO

VIA G. SACCONI

VIA DEI MALASPINA

CORSO MAZZINI

VIA DEI C. PICCOLOMINI

LA TANA DI PECOZ

L A TANA DI PECOZ

ASCOLI PICENO

In a few minutes, he returns to apologize for the delay in our first course, but our fresh *pennette agli aromi*—short, tubular noodles in a red pepper and tomato sauce—is well worth the brief wait. Next, Kevin and I share a platter of *carne alla brace*, a variety of meats—beef kabobs, lamb, and veal—grilled over an open-pit fire. The smoky flavor and aroma sate our appetites.

There's just enough room left for chocolate *gelati* (ice cream). Its soft texture and creamy cocoa flavor is a perfect ending.

By 9:30pm, we meander back to the square, where only a few couples are left, hiding in the romantic shadows. Tomorrow evening, the pre-dinner *passeggiata* will start again, and so will the race to La Tana Di Pecoz.

A Brief
Italian Lesson

My Italian is terrible, but I've managed to communicate well in Italy. On my first visit, I didn't try to speak the language. Although I knew a little, I was afraid. On a subsequent journey, Kevin and I traveled to remote areas where few people spoke English, forcing me to use what Italian I did know. The result was surprising—people understood me!

It didn't happen overnight. My method for communicating evolved over a week as I learned the tricks to this linguistic stuff. Armed with a handful of useful expressions, I conscientiously tried to talk like a native while asking for a hotel room or ordering food—like an actor playing a role. In stores, I'd eavesdrop on neighbors gossiping, then pick one word and speak it exactly as they did. They enunciate every syllable as if it were the most important sound in the world. At first I thought I sounded silly, but to a local, I sounded Italian.

Understanding Italians is easy once you realize you don't have to comprehend every word. One will do. I anticipated what the person was going to say based on the current situation, then listened for key words. So even if I didn't grasp three-quarters of the sentence (often the case), I guessed at the intent and answered accordingly, and 90% of the time I was right.

For instance, suppose a waiter approaches your table and begins clearing the plates. He looks at you and asks a question. You have no idea what he just said, but you did hear the word *secondo*. He's asking if you want a second course. It doesn't matter how he asked.

The important thing is you understood. If you do want to eat more, nod your head, if not, ask for the check. See how simple?

Be forewarned, though, that if you get too good at bluffing, Italians will think you're fluent, which could be embarrassing. One time in the Tuscan countryside, the owner of Trattoria La Sosta asked me to translate for an American couple at the next table. I'd had a liter of wine, so I thought the job seemed simple. But all I did was talk slower and louder—*in English!*—than the other English speakers. Everyone, including my husband, just stared at me like I was crazy.

There are times when I don't understand a word, so I smile brightly and use my "emergency" sentence, "*Sono una stupida Americana. Non parlo Italiano*" — "I'm a stupid American. I don't speak Italian." It always gets a laugh and lots of sympathy.

What follows is a brief lesson in Italian pronunciation and a group of phrases and words that will prove helpful. I promise—if you spend a few minutes to familiarize yourself with this beautiful language, you'll be richly rewarded. *Ciao!*

Consonants

b, d, f, k, l, m, n, p, q, t, v—same as English.

c—1) before "i" or "e", like "ch" in "cherry" (*citta*=city)
  2) elsewhere, like "c" in "can" (*casa*=house)

ch—like "k" in "kit" (*che*=what)

g—1) before "i" or "e", like "j" in "jump" (*gettone*=phone token)
  2) elsewhere, like "g" in "girl" (*gonna*=skirt)

gh—like "g" in "get" (*ghiaccia*=ice)

gli—like "lli" in "million" (*bottiglia*=bottle)

gn—like "ny" in "canyon" (*signore*=sir)

h—silent (*ho*=I have)

r—like "r" in "robe" with a slight trill (*ragazza*=girl)

s—usually like "s" in "see" (*sale*=salt), sometimes like "z" in "zoo"

sc—1) before "i" or "e", like "sh" in "shoe" (*schivo*=shy)
2) elsewhere, like "sk" in "skirt" (*scuola*=school)

z—usually like "ts" in "nuts" (*zio*=uncle), sometimes like "dz" in "roads" (*zero*=zero)

Vowels

a—like "a" in "star"

e—like "e" in "get"

i—like "ee" in "meet"

o—like "o" in "open"

u—like "oo" in "pool"

Useful Phrases for Dining

I would like—*Vorrei* (vohr-REH-ee)

to make a reservation—*fare una prenotazione* (FAH-reh oon-ah preh-noh-tah-tsee-OH-neh)

a table for two—*un tavolo per due* (oon TAH-voh-loh pehr DOO-eh)

the house wine—*vino della casa* (VEE-noh DAY-lah KAH-sah)

white wine—*vino bianco* (VEE-noh bee-AHN-koh)

red wine—*vino rosso* (VEE-noh ROHS-soh)

water (in Italy, it's preferable to purchase bottled water)—*acqua minerale* (AH-koo-ah mee-neh-RAH-leh)

a fork—*una forchetta* (oo-nah fohr-KAYT-tah)

a spoon—*un cucchiaio* (oon koo-key-AH-ee-oh)

a knife—*un coltello* (oon kohl-TEHL-loh)

a napkin—*un tovagliolo* (oon toh-vah-ly-ee-OH-loh)

dessert, sweets—*dolce* (DOHL-cheh)

the check—*il conto* (eel KOHN-toh)

Do you know a good *trattoria?*—*Conosce un buon trattoria?* (koh-NOH-sheh oon boo-OHN TRAHT-or-ee-ah)

What is it?—*Che cosa è?* (kay KOH-sah EH)

Where is the bathroom?—*Dov'è il bagno?* (doh-VEH eel BAH-ny-oh)

What is today's special?—*Qual è il piatto del giorno?* (koo-ah-LEH eel pee-AHT-toh dayl jee-OHR noh)

Is the kitchen open?—*È la cucina operto?* (eh lah koo-CHEE-nah ah-PEHR-toh)

Please speak slowly.—*Per piacere parli lentanente.* (pehr pee-ah-CHAY-reh PAHR-lee lehn-tah-MEHN-teh)

I don't understand.—*Non ho capito.* (nonhn oh kah-PEE-toh)

I'm American.—*Sono Americiano(a).* (SOH-noh ah-meh-re-KAH-noh/nah)

I'm finished.—*Ho finito.* (oh fee-NEE-toh)

Please—*Per favore* (pehr fah-VOH-reh)

Thank you—*Grazie* (GRAH-tsee-eh)

You're welcome—*Prego* (PREH-goh)

Good-bye/Hello—*Ciao* (chee-AH-oh)

Index to Regions, Towns, and Trattorie

(Towns in bold)

About the Author

Christina Baglivi's knowledge of Italian food and language comes directly from the kitchens of her grandfather Joseph Marasco, owner of La Grata Pizzeria, and her mother Rosemarie, who thought Christina was never too young to learn about a traditional Italian kitchen.

A native New Yorker, Christina won the Leonardo Da Vinci Award in 1978 for excellence in Italian patriotism, language, and culture. Now a resident of Los Angeles, she frequently writes travel articles for national magazines.

More Great Travel Books
from Mustang Publishing

Let's Blow thru Europe by Neenan & Hancock. The essential guide for the "15-cities-in-14-days" traveler, *Let's Blow thru Europe* is hilarious, irreverent, and probably the most honest guide to Europe ever written. Minor medieval cathedrals and boring museums? Blow 'em off! Instead, *Let's Blow* describes the key sites and how to see them as quickly as possible. Then, it takes you to the great bars, nightclubs, and restaurants that other guidebooks miss. *"Absolutely hilarious!"—Booklist.* **$10.95**

Europe on 10 Salads a Day by Mary Jane & Greg Edwards. A must for the health-conscious traveler! From gourmet Indian cuisine in Spain to terrific take-out pizza in Italy, this book details over 200 health-food/vegetarian restaurants throughout Europe. *"Don't go to Europe without it"—Vegetarian Times.* **$9.95**

Europe for Free by Brian Butler. If you think a trip to Europe will be a long exercise in cashing traveler's checks, then this is the book for you. **Europe for Free** describes *thousands* of fun things to see and do all over Europe—and nothing costs one single lira, franc, or pfennig. *"A valuable resource" —U.P.I.* **$8.95**

DC for Free by Brian Butler. The author of *Europe for Free* has turned his talent for finding freebies on America's capital, and the result is a money-saving guide to hundreds of free things to do and see all over Washington, DC and its suburbs. *"Packed with valuable information"—Senior Times.* **$6.95**

The Nepal Trekker's Handbook by Amy R. Kaplan. A trek through the magnificent mountains and villages of Nepal is one of the world's most exotic—yet relatively accessible—adventures. This book informs would-be trekkers about every aspect of planning and enjoying a healthy, fun trek. From what medicines to carry to cultural *faux-pas*, it's an essential guide. *"A must"—Midwest Book Review.* **$9.95**

Hawaii for Free by Frances Carter. How could anyone improve on Hawaii, America's paradise? Simple. Make a vacation there a whole lot cheaper! From free pineapple to free camping to a free brewery tour, this book describes hundreds of fun things to do throughout Hawaii—and nothing costs one penny. *"Invaluable" — Aloha Magazine.* **$6.95**

Australia: Where the Fun Is by Goodyear and Skinner. The "land down under" has become tops in travel, and these recent Yale graduates spent a year exploring both the tourist sites and the back alleys all over Australia. From the best pubs in Sydney to the cheapest motel in Darwin, this book details all the fun stuff—on and off the beaten path. *"Indispensable"—Library Journal.* **$12.95**
